# HIGH RISK SOLDIER:

## Trauma and Triumph in the Global War on Terror

By Terron Wharton

Copyright © 2016 by Terron Wharton
All rights reserved

ISBN-13: 978-1530402588

ISBN-10: 1530402581

For those suffering in silence

*I will always place the mission first.*
*I will never accept defeat.*
*I will never quit.*
*I will never leave a fallen comrade.*
-The Warrior Ethos from The Soldier's Creed

This book was written by Terron Wharton in his personal capacity. The opinions expressed in this book are the author's own and do not reflect the view of or endorsement by the United States Army, the Department of Defense, or the United States Government.

# Table of Contents

NOTES ON STRUCTURE, SPELLING, AND NAMES .................1
INTRODUCTION .................3
PROLOGUE .................7
IRAQ: FOB RUSTAMIYAH, BAGHDAD, IRAQ, OCTOBER 2006-JANUARY 2008 .................14
PART I: WELCOME TO COUNTRY .................15
PART II: DOWNHILL SLIDE .................59
PART III: BLOOD .................69
PART IV: THE WORST DAY .................83
PART V: GOING, GOING… .................105
PART VI: …GONE .................123
INTERLUDE: VICTORY BASE COMPLEX, BAGHDAD, IRAQ, JANUARY 2009 – JANUARY 2010 .................140
AFGHANISTAN: KANDAHAR CITY, KANDAHAR, AFGHANISTAN, APRIL 2012-JANUARY 2013 .................156
PART VII: BACK INTO THE BREACH .................157
PART VIII: COMMAND .................188
PART IX: THE LAST PUSH .................204
PART X: WHOLE AGAIN .................218
EPILOGUE .................225
ACKNOWLEDGEMENTS .................229
GLOSSARY .................231
ABOUT THE AUTHOR .................234

## Notes on structure, spelling, and names

What you are about to read is a collection of emails and journal entries I wrote over five years and three deployments. I edited the original entries to ease reading by removing jargon and unneeded acronyms. Additional editing cleaned up the manuscript to make it easier to read, while preserving the original feel and conversational tone. Acronyms used are found in the glossary.

Capitalization works a little differently for the military. You will see several words capitalized and not capitalized. Certain words like ranks, titles, and formations are capitalized based on whether they are being used as a proper noun or not. For example, if I'm talking about a random lieutenant, colonel, or unit commander (i.e. company commander) none of those would be capitalized. If I'm talking about a specific person or your unit commander, the words would be capitalized: The Lieutenant, the Company Commander, etc. The same goes for units and formations. "A battalion" is any random battalion, while Battalion (i.e. "The Battalion is heading south" or "Got a call from Battalion") refers to a specific unit, most likely your own or one you're reporting to.

Every detail may not be completely accurate. I wrote about some events right after they occurred. In other cases, it was days or weeks later before I could record them. Events may have happened at different times than I could recall. Other statements are based on my perspective from what I heard, saw, read, and experienced from events, reports, facts, and, yes, even rumors. There is a little of the blind man touching the elephant. I interpreted things based on my experiences, and that perspective, or lack thereof, gives insight into how events appeared at my level. What you read is what I remembered when I wrote it. In no way am I attempting to mislead, exaggerate, or be disingenuous.

I changed all names, units, hometowns, and other personal identifiable details to protect privacy. The events that happened in this book are still painful to many. However, fallen Soldiers names are mentioned to honor their service and sacrifice.

This is Our story as a brotherhood. The events, emotions, and feelings aren't exclusive to me or any other Soldier, Airman, Sailor, or Marine. If you've deployed and seen combat, you will have seen, felt, and gone through something similar. This book is for Us.

# **Introduction**

I was a "High Risk Soldier".

What follows is a story that will sound all too familiar these days. A service member goes to war, experiences horror and trauma, and comes back changed, drowning in depression, anger, nightmares, and substance abuse.

The Army's Soldier Leader Risk Reduction Tool (SLRRT) is used by Army leaders and supervisors to assess a Soldier's "Risk Level". A supervisor takes the form, sits the soldier down, and runs through a checklist of questions:

Has the Soldier engaged in risky behaviors?

Is the Soldier having relationship problems?

Is the Soldier having trouble sleeping?

Is the Soldier having difficulty coping with loss?

Has the Soldier expressed excessive anger or aggression?

Has the Soldier expressed suicidal thoughts or actions?

In typical Army fashion, the adjacent box gives "Leader Actions" to take if the Soldier answers yes to anything. At the end, the supervisor assesses the Soldier's "Risk Level" from low to high.

**Low Risk:** Soldier has no significant problems or has problems for which he/she is receiving appropriate support. The potential for adverse outcomes appears to be low.

**High Risk:** Behaviors or concerns that potentially place the Soldier or others in danger or harm's way (e.g., life threatening risk taking behavior, serious performance problems that jeopardize team members safety, threat to self or others). **Senior leadership (Battalion commander/equivalent or higher) and appropriate support channels should be notified immediately.**

While not always called SLRRT, some variation of a "Soldier Risk Assessment" has existed for most of the Global War on Terror. The Army wanted to help, but it was woefully unprepared for the sheer number of soldiers needing it. Unfortunately, high risk soldiers slipped through the cracks or, in some cases, were identified and not given the support needed. Too many times, these soldiers lost themselves to drugs, alcohol, depression, and suicide.

However, my story has a different ending.

I fought my problems. I sought help. I refused to quit.

My story has a simple message: You can fight it. You can beat it. Your pain isn't the end. Life gets better. Do not give up. Do not quit. You can make it.

I was a High Risk Soldier… and I am still standing.

*Halfway down the trail to Hell,
In a shady meadow green
Are the Souls of all dead troopers camped,
Near a good old-time canteen.
And this eternal resting place
Is known as Fiddler's Green.*

*Marching past, straight through to Hell
The Infantry are seen.
Accompanied by the Engineers,
Artillery and Marines,
For none but the shades of Cavalrymen
Dismount at Fiddler's Green.*

*Though some go curving down the trail
To seek a warmer scene.
No trooper ever gets to Hell
Ere he's emptied his canteen.
And so rides back to drink again
With friends at Fiddler's Green.*

*And so when man and horse go down
Beneath a saber keen,
Or in a roaring charge of fierce melee
You stop a bullet clean,
And the hostiles come to get your scalp,
Just empty your canteen,
And put your pistol to your head
And go to Fiddler's Green*
-Fiddler's Green, an old Cavalry poem


*And so when you're on the road
And catch an IED
Or walking round while on patrol
And a sniper stops you clean*

*When haji starts to overrun*
*Just empty your canteen*
*And put your pistol to your head*
*And go to Fiddler's Green*
　　-Added by guys in my unit written during my time in Baghdad

# **Prologue**

When I was a junior in high school my parents sat me down for a talk. It went a little something like this:

"We have no money for college."

"What? How? I thought you guys had started a college fund years ago or something?"

"Oh no, no, no. We spent that on private school so YOU could pay for college."

That short exchange shaped the rest of my life. Two types of people lived in my hometown: those who grew up and never left and those who grew up and never came back. I wasn't exactly born on the wrong side of the tracks, but it was only one bad life choice away. I recognized early on that my town held little opportunity for me. I had to get out.

My interest in the military started early in high school. I joined the JROTC program and got heavily involved in drill team and other clubs associated with the program. As a sophomore, about 15, I read Colin Powell's book *My American Journey*. It changed my life. Serving was no longer a passing interest. This is what I wanted to do. No, this is what I was MEANT to do. For me the Army was not a job or even a career. It was a calling.

Like most kids growing up in Indiana, I looked at Indiana University as a college option. I also looked at MIT, Johns Hopkins, Tufts, and some others. Then I looked at the price tags for MIT, Johns Hopkins, Tufts, and some others. Wherever I went, I would have to get a full ride. My dad's a career police officer and my mom was a partner in a small business. They could not afford to help me. Tuition, room, board, and living expenses would all be on me.

One of my JROTC Instructors, SFC Tomlin, retired from Army Special Forces. SFC Tomlin recognized my potential and became a mentor. During one detention (hey, what can I say? I wasn't a saint) he talked to me about college while I cleaned the armory. He asked if I had ever considered going to West Point. I looked confused. I had only heard about West Point because of the Army-Navy game. I had no clue what it was about, what it was like, and had never considered applying.

As high school progressed, things started looking up for me. I was a varsity athlete, the head of our JROTC program, and an honors student. I ended up receiving a full academic scholarship to Indiana University and an offer to West Point. I reasoned that if I went to Indiana University I would still have expenses, even with a stipend. Still wild in my youth, civilian school held the temptation to party and chase women, ultimately causing me to lose focus. However, West Point would instill discipline. More importantly, West Point is paid for. Even if I blew my stipend, all basic needs were still met. Based on all the stupid crap I pulled in high school I have no I idea how I made that type of mature decision. Thank God I was smarter than myself at that moment.

On July 2, 2001, I reported to R-Day with the rest of the class of 2005. On July 3rd I was standing in formation and freezing my ass off in the frigid Hudson Valley morning thinking I had made a monumental mistake. Going to West Point was kind of like going to combat for the first time. You go into it eyes wide open because you're too dumb to realize what you're getting yourself into. Beast Barracks went by in a blur of sweat, yelling, and constant memorization. Don't ask me how many gallons are in Lusk Reservoir. I never learned it then and I sure as hell never looked it up afterwards.

Then on September 11, 2001, things changed forever. I was getting ready for my class when my team leader threw open my door and screamed to turn on the TV. I saw the World Trade Center on fire. I ran outside and saw people running everywhere. MPs were staking sandbags and entry points. Machine guns set up to defend the post. Trucks with .50 cals patrolled the road. I heard the sonic boom overhead of two jets racing down the Hudson to New York. When I reached Thayer Hall every classroom looked the same: cadets and instructors all glued to the TV. I watched the second tower fall. As the smoke billowed my instructor said something I will never forget:

"This day will change and define your lives forever."

Despite the ominous prediction West Point wasn't always work. I drank in life like only a 20 year old with their whole life in front of them can. I spent my pass weekends in New York City, stomping around The Village, Times Square, and Spanish Harlem. A tiny apartment in upper Manhattan was a frequent destination, Maria's mom making beans and rice while the rest of the crew dances to salsa in the living. Another night we slept like bums inside Grand Central Station because we missed the last train to where we were staying. A favorite memory involved stumbling out of Webster Hall at 6 am, my best friend and I running like mad so we don't miss the ferry back to Stanton Island. I believe he referred to that incident as "racing the sun." My time off was a kaleidoscope of club music, cherry swisher sweets, and laughter spent with friends who had become family.

As a senior I assigned as battalion commander, I still managed to become a regular at the Firstie Club drinking cheap beer and playing pool with my friends. My battalion knew they would have relaxed room standards every Friday because I was too hung over from Friday night to bother cleaning. However, I am proud to say that my roommate only had to hold me up by my pistol belt during morning formation a single time... That I can recall. I was carefree, a jokester. I became slightly (in)famous as a rabble rouser and a joker, keeping a blog of experiences. I shared it and would often post irreverent quips to my AIM (Yes, AIM. I'm dating myself) profile... a blog the academy eventually found out about my senior year... that resulted in me walking hours... as a cadet battalion commander.

Even with the fun, West Point was challenging. At times I didn't think I would make it, especially when I was struggling with math or getting tutoring for survival swimming. Yes, you heard that right. I went to tutoring for swimming. By some freak accident I ended up in the intermediate class instead of the "you'll drown without floaties" class. I passed by the skin of my teeth and my instructor's pity. Three things kept me going: My desire to fight, my sense of humor, and my friends. Despite the seriousness of the situation, we were still college kids. Well, we were college kids in a pressure cooker. Academics, stress, high standards, and a competitive environment are not what most 18 year olds think college will be like. On top of it all, the war constantly loomed in the background.

The Global War on Terror came to define my entire time at the academy. It was more than a drive to succeed. I was committed before. Now, I was a true believer. I couldn't wait to graduate. We hoped the war wasn't over before we got our chance to fight. It was all we talked about. I planned to go combat arms so I could be on the front line destroying America's enemies.

Eventually, on May 28, 2005 I graduated. My Regimental TAC Officer hugged me and said "I'm so happy you're graduating." I still haven't figured out if she was happy for me or happy she no longer had to deal with my antics. 911 of us walked across the stage that day. 911 excited, wide eyed, true believers. We were on way.

After my basic course I got assigned to a combined arms battalion in the Cav at Fort Hood. I reported in the middle of a field problem and met my platoon during evening LOGPAC. I had hit the ground as the unit just started training up for Iraq. It seemed like every couple of months we were in the field. Lanes, gunnery, more lanes, NTC, another gunnery, more lanes. I had the dream train up for a deployment. We trained constantly, mastering the basics, coming together, molding ourselves together into a single, living weapon.

When I wasn't training I spent time with my impromptu family. I had several good friends stationed at Fort Hood with me. I'd often have them over to my tiny apartment, music playing, "grilling" for everyone on my tiny George Foreman, and enjoying each other. I also met Sara. The mutual attraction was magnetic and I fell in love before I knew it. Knowing our deployments were fast approaching we spent every moment we could together. I remember talking for hours, listening to music, and drinking cheap beers. I remember coming home from the field to find her waiting in my apartment to surprise me... only to have the reunion temporarily halted by the reek of cordite and fuel coming off of my body. I remember writing her love letters under a starry sky while I trained at NTC. I remembered trying to savor every sensation, the smell of her hair, the way her eyes crinkled when she laughed, and the way she felt cuddled against me. I remember the day she deployed. I saw her off with a brave face only to cry for the rest of the night.

    I loved her. My God, I loved that woman. I loved her like I would never love again. She was my all. My whole world. My reason for being. I was sure of two things in my life: American righteousness in the GWOT and that Sara would be my wife. My life was going exactly how I'd planned. Everything was coming together for me. I could hardly believe how lucky I'd gotten. I was barely 23, but I had found my dream career and the love of my life. The rest of my life waited just around the corner. All I had to do was get through the deployment. We deploy, come back, and start our life together. I was sure. I was so damn sure.

# Iraq:
# FOB Rustamiyah, Baghdad, Iraq
# October 2006-January 2008

# Part I:
# Welcome to Country

On October 23, 2006 I left Fort Hood and headed to Kuwait for my first deployment. We had been hearing for a while that we'd be heading to FOB Falcon, the same place the Battalion was stationed during their first deployment. Instead, we found out, just before leaving, that we were heading to a place called FOB Rustamiyah, which sat on the Eastern Side of Baghdad at the Southern end of RTE Plutos just south of where it intersects RTE Brewers.

All I could think of that last night in the States was going to war. I was going to combat! All of the waiting, the training, the endless hours of practice, and I was FINALLY going to get to do it for real! Would I be able to? Would I freeze up? Could I lead men under fire? I would soon find out. With Sara already gone, the rest of my friends at Fort Hood (we'd formed a little extended family) gathered to send me off.

As I said, Sara deployed to Baghdad a couple months before me and was stationed at Victory Base Complex on the western side of the city. To my delight, she met me when I flew up from Kuwait. My last happy memory before heading to Rustamiyah was sneaking behind a tent with Sara to steal a kiss under a clear, moonlit desert sky.

That kiss possessed a finality that I didn't truly understand at the time. It was a kiss full of love, longing, and sorrow. It was a true kiss goodbye. Neither of us knew it yet, but that was the last either of us would ever see of the man I used to be.

### Journal: October 24, 2006 (Day 2)

Arrived in Kuwait late in the night after traveling for God only knows how long. Too many flights, too many time zones, not enough natural sleep... it feels hazy... like my brain is trying to operate in sludge. So here I sit on my cot, day 1 of 365. Come on boys! We're going to war! ...But for what? For who? This is not my country, my people, or my fight. Of course we know the party line: We're here to bring democracy and freedom to the Iraqi people and stop the spread of terrorism. The bigger question is, so what?

What makes a person turn left instead of right, choose this path instead of that one? How did I go from wanting to study genetics in high school to sitting in a tent in the middle of the Kuwaiti desert as an officer in the United States Army? Don't ask me, because right now, I sure as hell can't give you a concrete answer. Then there's always the greater question attached to that one: Do you want to be here?

The short answer is not only no, but hell no! No one in their right mind wants to leave friends, family, love, and home for this God-Forsaken shit hole on the far side of the earth. Why in the hell would you be excited to get shot at? There really is no plausible reason. So why am I here? To prove to myself I can do it. To prove to myself I have what it takes to lead men under fire and win. Hell, I may not do half bad... or I could buy it on the first run out the gate. Who knows?

But it's too easy to use that as an excuse for the reason I'm here. I guess.... It's because it feels natural and I love my job. Even though I can't quite shake the gnawing fear in my belly... still, the only people who aren't afraid are liars and fools. So here I sit, about to hit dirt in Iraq in a week, trying to wrap my head around finally being here. Trying to let home go, trying to let go of all the last phone calls, and trying to find a way to put myself away in a box so as not to be damaged beyond repair when I return. I guess only time will tell, but I sure as hell wish time would hurry the fuck up.

### Journal: November 3, 2006 (Day 13)

Been stuck in Iskandariyah for the last 3 days. This place is a shit hole. It's everything you'd think a war zone should be minus the burning vehicles and dead bodies. Too many days of travel and nicotine coupled with not enough food or sleep have left a sense of surreal detachment. I take another drag on my thousandth cigarette and let the smoke curl out of my mouth, over my lips, and into my nose. I got lucky enough to see Sara for a couple hours over at the BIAP. It was the highlight of my year. I can just see us telling that story to the kids. Too many cigarettes and not enough sleep… too many cigarettes and not enough sleep.

### Journal: November 25, 2006 (Day 35)

It's been crazy these last few weeks. I barely have any sense of time, place, what I'm doing, where I'm going. It's all one big blur of patrols, taskings, briefings, and restrictions. The Battalion Commander pulled all the Platoon Leaders and Platoon Sergeants in for a meeting the other week. He wanted the "guys on the ground" to give their opinion. He wanted to remind us that we're not "combat soldiers" but "police officers" and if necessary a "swat team." The last time I checked cops weren't getting blown up by roadside bombs or getting their heads chopped off by the local criminals. I must have missed the memo that stated I'm not combat fucking arms.

And none of this makes the six o'clock...

Mortars hit the FOB, 17 got blown up the other day, a sniper whacks an MP on the road and another dies on a hospital bed. Guys getting smoked left and right in this bitch. And it's raw, and it's gritty, and the stench of sewage and blood and rage fills your nostrils. You look out the corner of your eyes and think "Fuck these Iraqis, let me go home and let them tear each other's throats out." But then you shake hands with a child. Then you sit down in a man's house and have dinner with his family and blow smoke rings to make his baby girl giggle. Then you meet the guys who are just trying to get by day to day, fuck the politics. But none of this makes the six o'clock.

And none of this makes the CNN news ticker. Talking about Dave Matthews Band while you sit clammed up in your tank on a checkpoint for seven hours, your hatch barely cracked to allow air in, and your cigarette down behind the rim of the hatch cause the snipers will key on the cherry. The stench of stale sweat.... None of that gets on the six o'clock.

Neither does the fact that the building I live in has a tin roof and we take mortars all the time. Neither does the fact that my lungs are choked daily on the sand, and dust, and thick smoke from whatever just exploded or caught fire.... Neither does drinking a near beer that tastes like piss just because you want something, ANYTHING, that reminds you of a shred of the life you used to have. None of that goes on the six o'clock.

Neither do the three day stretches of patrol, patrol, patrol. No one hears about the five hours of sleep that's interrupted by mortar fire landing right behind your building. Nothing's reported on you and 50 of your closest mates press into a tiny bunker for shelter, switching between flipping birds and cracking jokes at JAM's shitty shooting and huddling closer when one lands too near. Neither does too many cigarettes and not enough sleep, bleary eyes peering in thermal sights, or packs of wild dogs chasing your tank at night. None of that gets on the six o'clock.

No, none of this war really gets on the six o'clock. Nothing but the snippets, the sound bites, the convenient, sexy shots someone hopes will win them a Pulitzer. The Soldier... the real war... is never on the six o'clock.

## Journal: November 26, 2006 (Day 36)

Too much nicotine, not enough sleep. Too much sitting and waiting and not enough adrenaline. My system needs a shutdown, reboot, and a juice... redo the wiring, up the response, bleed out the lag... God I just want to go home. I wake up every day to the crushing reality that yes, this place is my home for a year. I guess it's better now that we're up and running hard. Little time except for wake, smoke, eat, smoke, shit, smoke, prep, smoke, brief, smoke, mission, smoke, smoke, smoke, debrief, smoke, eat, smoke, sleep. I wonder what my parents are doing. I wonder what real beer tastes like... I wonder if I should publish this. In case you don't read the news, war shit is pretty hot right now. I could probably get a nice chunk for a stream-of-consciousness war journal. In that case, I better start writing more about my feelings. People always assume soldiers in a combat zone have all the "deep thoughts" about the mission, their family, God, Corp, and Country. Hell, all I want to do is get through the next day and come one step closer to home. Actually, I just want to make it to the next meal without my legs giving out. Heh, marking time by meals… I haven't done that since West Point…… 12 bells and all is well, another day in my little brown cell, another day all shot to hell, ah well. And none of this gets on the six o'clock.

### Email: November 30, 2006 (Day 40)

So here's the current news from over here. I got promoted the other day to 1st Lieutenant along with the rest of my classmates from school. My gunner and BN CDR pinned me between patrols, so moments after I got pinned I had to go back out the gate.... almost two hours late. There was an amazing coincidence of events that kept us from going out the gate on time, and we all came to the agreement God was trying to tell us something about not going out on patrol that night... which ended in a massive failure of commo… and navigation systems. I lead the way deaf, mute, and blind back to the FOB. Oh yeah, did I mention the locals like to block off streets with wire and barriers? Streets open the previous day? Randomly guessing a route is not the preferred method to escape a maze of dead ends and blocked roads. It was a sweet trip.

In other news, the rolling commo blackouts that prevented my contact with the outside world are finally done. A commo blackout is when the command shuts down all internet and phones. They do it when someone is seriously injured or killed so the family can be officially notified instead of finding out through a random phone call or Facebook post. They've been going on since before Thanksgiving, so I had to sneak a call home for that one. Sara and I are definitely glad we can talk a little more regularly now as opposed to an hour every two to three days.

And here is a little more on my living conditions. Feel free to pass this on to people who think that soldiers just love to travel far away and oppress other people. I live in what could basically be described as a shoebox. The room itself is pretty big... but I split it between me, my platoon sergeant, and my platoon office/storage space. So, my wall is comprised of wall lockers, and my door is a sheet hanging from rope line. I have no heat, and whoever told me it's always hot in the desert all year round is a liar. It dropped to freezing last night, and I slept in everything from long underwear to my comforter, to the quillow Mrs. Smith sent me (thank you so much), and a couple of sheets I could dig up. The walls are paper thin, so you can hear everything that goes on. I have one power outlet as the other hangs from the wall and occasionally shoots sparks. The best thing about where I live is the showers are only 10 ft away and usually have a good supply of hot water. It could be worse.

I don't talk about my politics very much, so all I'll say is this. This country will not get better until we leave. I hate this place, and I've only been here a month. At least I'm making decent pay. Still, it's hard to justify going out the gate everyday to fight a war with both hands and feet tied behind your back and your rules of engagement are more to cover the asses of politicians and generals than a guideline for your soldiers. Ah well, things always could be worse. This could be Vietnam, right?

**Journal: December 3, 2006 (Day 43)**

Sitting here in Iraq once again dreaming of cigarette smoke, black skullies, storefronts at midnight, and dancing in the parking lot listening to punk rock. Happier times, happy memories, some of the best moments in my life. No cares, no worries, just us, just each other. What I wouldn't give to go back to one of those summers now, trading it for this. I saw the Brigade Commander at dinner tonight. I talked to him and gave the general line; "We're tired and shorthanded sir, but we're holding strong." I sat down with my coffee, lowered my head, sighed heavily, and rubbed my eyes hard, and when I looked up, he was standing there with genuine concern in his eyes. "Hang in there, Wharton, you can make it."

Hang in there, Wharton, you can make it. Hang in there, Wharton. Hang in where? To what? What am I fighting for? Why am I here? I wake up every day and ask myself what I believe in over here. The answer most days is nothing. I don't believe in a damn thing over here. Still, I keep telling myself that if I can affect positive change in one person's life here the year will be worth it. In reality…. Is it? I bought propane for a family that lives in the OP building and it made me feel good inside… but is it worth the risk to my own life and that of my Soldiers?

Disillusionment sets in one cold trickle at a time, and once again I'm forced to grow up much faster than I ever wanted. I'm forced to balance command, feelings, my humanity, my sanity…

What is the point of this war? We trumpet the ideals of "freedom" and "democracy" to the public and media. We say Iraq will be better with free elections, but are they really free? True freedom is the ability to say with conviction "I choose" and have the force of will to make that choice manifest in the flesh. Isn't true freedom the ability to choose subjugation? What matters, the form of government? The only thing that matters, the only thing that truly defines freedom, is the choice itself, whatever the fruits of that choice may be. The choice itself is the fruit of freedom, not the products of the choice. Freedom is only lost when the choice is stripped away unwillingly.

So where does that leave me? In reality, what I do here will most likely not make one iota of difference. And none of this matters to the press or politicians except as ratings, poll numbers, and campaign ammunition. Bring our troops home! There's no direction in this war! But do they really care, or is it just the election season rally cry? How many folded flags have they received? How many weeping mothers have they seen? How many letters of condolence have they written to crying children? How many times have they waited for a phone call, wondering if it will ever come?

And I pour out my heart, and I pour out my soul, and I pour out my blood, and I pour out my hate, and my rage, and my anger, and my tears, and my life… and none of it produces one bit of change, and none of it makes any difference to the people in charge. One thing is for damn sure: all I want is to go home.

### **Email: December 3, 2006 (Day 43)**

Just got off a 24 hour observation post (OP) in the middle of Baghdad. Translation: I sat on a roof, peered through binoculars, listened to a radio, and froze my ass off. It wasn't all that bad though. The neighborhood kids came up and brought us chai. At dinner they hauled up a pot of homemade chicken and vegetables, bread, and cheese. I gave the kid money to buy his family propane as they didn't have any. Before the war propane was about

$0.50 a tank. Now it's $15. We're not going to crush the insurgency, run Sadr out into the desert, and make Iraq a true democracy... but if I can do one good thing for one person that sticks, then it will be worth it for me, cause we all know I damn sure don't do it for the pay.

Sara and I got promoted to First Lieutenant on 28 Nov (I can't remember if I said this already... everything kind of runs together here), and the highlight of yesterday had to be getting her letter in the mail with a Polaroid of her in it. I now have a picture for my room to accompany the one I've had folded in my wallet since the desert at the National Training Center. Thanks, baby. It's a strange thing to be deployed at the same time as your significant other. You lose track of when you talk, for how long, what's happened since the last time you did. You try to catch each other up without depressing each other with what's going on. You fight with the phone for five minutes of decent reception and then hang up and wonder when the next time you'll get to talk, trying not to think how that may be the last time. As I told one of my Soldiers who complained while on OP yesterday: "You forgot there are people out here who want nothing more than to kill you?"

I may not trust that being over here is the right thing to do, but you have to find something to have faith in when in a place like this. Something more than mere survival. So yes, while I have never believed that human beings are capable of true altruism, I still buy into a part of it. You'd have to be a cold-hearted bastard not to feel good inside when a kid tears up in gratitude for the propane you bought his family. We all need something to hold on to. Even if I don't believe in altruism, I can still use it to find my one good thing.

### Email: December 9, 2006 (Day 49)

This war isn't a war in the traditional sense. You know, massed armies clashing on open plains, soldiers on foot charging to take the hill, that sort of thing. No, if you want to see what this war is like, turn on Spike TV and watch Cops... I'm serious. We're more akin to the NYPD than combat arms soldiers. The other day we pulled two guys over for violating curfew. Now mind you, these guys had weapons in their car and on them with no permits. So do me and my boys run out of the trucks with rifles flying and butt strokes to the head? Nope. I'm questioning these guys, checking IDs, checking vehicle registration and plate numbers.... I was tempted to ask for proof of insurance and quip "Do you know how fast you were going?" And just like Cops, my other guys were busy holding back the knot of people gathering in curiosity saying things like "Mister, mister, he good guy." Seriously, I almost expected some Iraqi woman in a nighty, flip-flops, and a black eye to walk out of a nearby house and start yelling "Told you not to hit me again, asshole! Take him to jail!"

We're police, except we don't get to carry Tasers or night sticks. The guys we stopped were shady as fuck with some shady stuff in their car, but it wasn't enough to arrest them... yeah, not enough to arrest them. This is not OIF I or II where you could snatch a guy for just looking at you funny. Hell, even the POLICE can snatch a guy and put him in lock up if he gets mouthy.., and New Yorkers aren't leaving roadside bombs for the NYPD. We have to justify and collect evidence, because if not it's an international incident. So I go out every night on my beat, rolling around and chasing ghosts, trying not to get blown up. Oh yeah, I found out our trucks definitely stop bullets. Iraqi police think firing in the air to clear traffic is a good idea.

I've only been here for less than 2 months it feels like 6 already... only 10 and a half more to go.

## **Email: December 14, 2006 (Day 54)**

Just got off of another shift in my tank at the ole' checkpoint and one thing is for sure: I'm tired as hell and my back is killing me. It's been a rough few days of not enough sleep, no kind of steady sleep cycle (or any biorhythm), and way too many changes with too little notice. Just another typical day in East Baghdad. Between being bored to tears and slipping into madness while crammed into my metal shoebox for another 7 hours, I got to thinking.

Soldiers are trained to fight, or, as the manual says, "close with and destroy the enemy." What is this war like? Imagine being in a boxing match where both hands are tied behind your back and your opponent can hit you in the face all you want. Now and then the ref will untie you and let you take one swing, but before you can the other guy has moved halfway across the ring. Once in a while, if you're LUCKY, the other guy will be stupid enough to stay in range so you can get one good shot. That's what this war is. We don't want to kill, we want to HIT BACK. We took a 30 round mortar and rocket barrage the other day. Sitting huddled in the bunker waiting for the next one to hit we hoped and prayed that someone higher up would finally let our mortar guys shoot back. They did... five rounds.

Soldiers are trained to fight, and when the stress, frustration, and unspent aggression build up with no enemy to take it out on, it turns in on itself. Short tempers, mood disorders, insomnia, squabbling, drugs, alcohol... it all stems from frustration, frustration of never being able to give it as good as you're taking it. High intensity conflict, while probably more terrifying, has to be much easier. You can see your enemy, you can kill your enemy, you can take something tangible away... this, what I live in, is like trying to hold on to smoke. You're always five minutes too late, one block too far over... he's always already across the ring. Couple that to a sense of perpetual physical and mental exhaustion and the never ending repetition of living the same day over and over. In case you had any misconceptions:

WAR

NEVER

STOPS

    I hear Sara tell me how her one day off a week never seems to happen. How she can't remember the last time she got a full day to herself to rest. I sit with my tank commanders and see how we can rest our guys. We try to shoot for 12 hours between checkpoint shifts, but here's the deal, that isn't 12 hours off. It's 12 hours BETWEEN MISSIONS. For example, you get off at 8 AM and you roll again at 8 PM. 1 hour at the start is gone for fueling the tanks, shutting the systems down, etc. 11 hours. One hour is taken for pre-mission prep on the other end. Ten hours. Factor in 2 hours for hygiene, food, errands (laundry, taskings, etc.). Eight hours. There, you can get a full 8 hours of sleep... if that's all you do. You forget about maintenance, meetings, emergencies that come up, the mortar attacks that happen just as you fall asleep. So, if you're lucky you may get 6 hours of actual free time for sleep or whatever. But like I said, 12 hours in between is the goal... it's commonly six. Bye-bye sleep. We don't get weekends, we don't get holidays. We measure time off in hours... hours that are usually eaten up by one thing or another. War never stops. Ever.

## Email: December 20, 2006 (Day 60)

So I just got back from a day long mission escorting Kurds down to Iskandariyah so they could pick up equipment. It was supposed to be a 24 hour plus mission, but we got it done in 15 hours, 9 minutes. Yes, I ran a stopwatch. It's amazing the motivation you can dig up when the driving factor is "eating something not out of a plastic pouch for once." So, hopped up on caffeine, sugar, and who knows how much nicotine, my boys and 1st Platoon moved a 71 vehicle convoy over 70 kilometers through Baghdad.

Dealing with Iraqis and Kurds is like dealing with a bunch of grown, heavily armed, five year olds. They wander off, ignore what you say, go when they feel like, stop when they aren't supposed to, lack any discipline, and are a general pain in the ass. This is magnified when your Battalion gives you interpreters who don't speak Kurdish... For those of you not familiar with Arabic and Kurdish, it's like Spanish to our English: Same alphabet (mostly), same writing (kind of), a lot of words even sound the same and you may be able to pick out one or two... but can you actually communicate with each other without knowing the other language? Exactly. At one point, there was a break in the Kurdish section because when the convoy took off, the next driver decided to stop and get out to take a leak. So, when the other section goes out of sight (down a road that is perfectly straight with one bend in it where the other part of the convoy is stopped waiting) does he drive forward? No, he sits there... for 15 minutes.... until I move one of my trucks in front of him and drive him back up to the rest of the convoy.... and when we motion for him to go past, he stays behind us... even after we wave him around.... and this is just one painful incident. It was like being a sheepherder, except the sheep have guns and twitchy trigger fingers. While on FOB Falcon a few of the Kurds refused to go any further because it was getting dark and they were tired and hungry and they didn't want to eat MREs... until their own leaders pulled guns on them and told them to move. It seems like violence is one of the few universally understood languages across human culture.

## **Email: December 20, 2006 (Day 60)**

I can't sleep. Normally, a soldier given five minutes and a place to sit can drift off with ease. It's one thing you learn to do. And now, given a bed, blankets, and a dark room I can't fall asleep. It's most likely because my sleep cycle has been so screwed up for the last two weeks. I talked to a friend of mine who's finishing officer's basic and got the whole "I can't wait to deploy" mentality I found myself in a few months ago. No one wants to be left back home and miss their shot at "the action." It's normal. Imagine playing football and always practicing but never getting to play a game. This is our game, and no one wants to be on the bench while everyone else is playing. Everyone wants their combat patch.

When I was younger, I remember my father telling me "don't be in a rush to grow up, these are the best times of your life." I took this long to realize he was right. I would give anything to freeze time back in July when I was back at Hood with my family. Me, Sara, Jim and Katie, Mike and Tammy, Aimee, Clara... ever since I left for the army, it was the first time in my life I felt like I had a home again. Fort Wayne and my parents will always be my home, but once you take off on your own it can take a while for a new place to fill the void. I miss those times. I miss running off with Jim and Mike, getting into all sorts of things, and then going "ok, what are we going to tell the girls." I miss cooking for the gang in the apartment. I miss seeing Sara. For the life of me, I can't figure out why I was in a hurry to deploy and get my combat patch. Deployment makes you appreciate the little things. One of my tank commanders and I were in the PX today and couldn't even find a coffee mug. Something so simple you could find in a gas station back home you can't find here.

Sara told me that John Kerry was at Victory tonight, and it got me thinking. The last people Soldiers want visits from in a war zone are politicians, regardless of stance, party affiliation, etc. Why? It means we have to drastically alter our lives, lose sleep and free time, and be stuffed into the location so it can all look pretty for the camera, then give "proper answers" when asked "How are you doing, Soldier?" and "How's the war going?' and, my favorite, "Do you think the U.S. should leave Iraq?" What does PVT Snuffy say? "Why no, sir, we should stay till the fight is done! We need more forces so we can accomplish the mission"... because they're briefed that if they don't say that or say something they truly feel (like "I just want to go home to my wife and kids instead of riding around waiting to get blown up because that's all we're doing over here") then they'll be on extra duty filling sandbags for a week in full gear. Who do Soldiers want to see? Their families. If they flew families over and back, heck, you could send the boys charging across the desert for a week on the morale boost.

## Journal: December 27, 2006 (Day 67)

The early morning of December 27th started out like any other I've had at Rusty. I woke up at the crack of dawn for an early morning mission only to discover that the power had once again gone out in the middle of the night, leaving the room pitch-black and freezing. The power was also down in the Company Command Post, so I grunted, swore under my breath at the loss of a hot cup of coffee, and lit a second cigarette out in the freezing cold. The mission for the morning was one I'd run before again and again: heavy cordon for the infantry while they searched the neighborhood. Move in, set up, and try not to fall asleep as I sit there bored to tears while the grunts kicked in doors and (hopefully) find something that warrants a local coming back in cuffs. Just another boring routine day. I wondered how long it would be before I'd be back warm in my rack. I wondered what Sara was doing. I planned out the rest of my day. I wondered if I'd get mail. I wondered if someone would be stupid enough to shoot at my tank and make our day. We have a lot of pent-up frustration to get out.

These were the things on my mind as I rounded the corner onto Route Florida and started the final approach to the objective. I scanned the area and looked at my CITV screen with half interest, concentrating more on how I would get us set up around the objective and, most importantly, trying to stay awake. MRE coffee grounds washed down with Mountain Dew and followed with three cigarettes was a poor substitute for sleep.

At 0530 on December 27th I was 200 meters from making the last turn to get to the objective when I got blown up. I was looking out the vision blocks when I saw the flash, had enough time for my mind to get out "Oh fu-" and that was it. My next coherent moment found me shoved against the turret wall at an odd angle, my body half wrapped around the Tank Commander's control handle, my hand keying the radio, and my voice yelling out the contact report. My wingman and I accelerated out of the kill zone and set up security. The bomb was a big one, and, miraculously, our tank shrugged it off and kept moving. I don't remember the next few minutes after the explosion. My sole concern was we were alive and the tank could still roll. All I remember was the explosion, the shock, and the subsequent anger when my wingman lost the triggermen between buildings just before ripping them to pieces with his machine gun. The infantry got out of their Bradleys to search the area and asked the Iraqi Police (who were sitting 50m from the blast sight watching it) some questions. I was happy to hear they didn't ask nicely. We ran through the standard procedures: move out the kill zone, set up security, damage assessment, regroup, continue mission. No one was dead. We were lucky.

In fact, we had been really lucky. My Platoon Sergeant pulled alongside my tank to check out the damage and I could see the shock register on his face. Our tank was done. I don't mean, take her back to the motor pool for repairs and back out in a week or a month done. I mean back to the motor pool to be cannibalized for parts and then shipped off to a state side depot level of done. An EFP had struck our tank. An EFP is basically a simple shape charge. It's a lot of explosives packed into a cylinder with a copper plate sealing it inside. When it blows, the charge inverts the copper disc and turns it into a poor man's sabot round, using the shape and speed to punch through armor.

The big ones are the tank killers. Thankfully they're relatively rare due to the cost, size and weight. They're also hard to move and set up with any sort of speed. The tank killers are typically set up in advance or have been in place for some time waiting on a good target. By the grace of God, the EFP missed the fuel cell. Someone could have died. Instead, we got bumps and bruises, the worst off being me with a bad concussion. I'll be rolling again in two days.

God continued to watch over us. We limped the tank back across 16 kilometers of neighborhoods and highway that was getting busy with early morning traffic. It was just me and my wingman. Had we gotten hit again we wouldn't have been able to maneuver or recover the vehicles without external help, and had our left track given out (how it stayed intact and didn't snap in the blast is still beyond me) we'd have had no one to watch our backs while we tried to fix it. When I finally saw the damage up close in the daylight I couldn't help feeling amazed.

I want to take the last of this email to say one thing: I love you all and each of you is special to me. We don't say that to each other enough in our lives, and I want to make sure I say this now while I still have the chance. Once again, we're all ok. I got my bell rung pretty bad and blacked out for a split second, but that's all. I'm going back out to find these guys and their buddies and show them my gratitude. Hopefully, we'll get a break and I'll be able to express my feelings in a personal way. I miss you guys.

**Email: January 3, 2007 (Day 74)**

This has been an incredibly boring week. We have the checkpoint mission this week which means one thing: sit in the tank for eight hours and stare at the screen for your optics. Yep, that's it. Sit and watch for eight hours. Every couple of hours we'll take a little jaunt down the road to mix it up, but it pretty much involves sitting still. Think of it like a police stakeout, but instead of donuts, coffee, and stale cigarette smoke in a hotel room, it's more like

Gatorade, MREs, and stale cigarette smoke in a big metal box. Oh yeah, and Iraq gets cold (I saw a frozen puddle this morning) and while the tank does have a nice heater, it usually ends up roasting the driver and gunner and as soon as you turn it off it's freezing again. Apparently the big metal box acts as a fridge in the winter and an oven in the summer.... So yeah, to compound the boredom further, I work the graveyard shift, so there is NOTHING going on... except for the dog fights. Nothing like watching packs of wild dogs fight for food on the highway to kill a few hours. Last night I came up with a list of things to do to keep occupied while on the checkpoint and during deployment.

How to Stay Occupied at the Checkpoint:

1. Watch wild dogs fight over food.
2. Play chicken with local traffic.
2a. The tank usually wins.
3. Yell odd thing at people down your gun tube. It acts like a megaphone!
4. Moon the houses bordering the road (yes, someone in another Company did this).
5. Follow neighborhood children around with the gun tube.
6. Pull a moped over with your tank (Yeah, I did that one).
6a. Bonus points if the guy freaks out and falls off (yep, that was me too... in all fairness he was breaking curfew).
7. Watch the Iraqis at the police checkpoints pick their noses in the guard tower.
8. Race the tanks down the highway. Got mine up to 40 mph.
9. Block traffic for no good reason.
10. Do donuts on the highway in your tank.
11. Rig a slingshot to the breach and use it to shoot rocks at things and belligerent pedestrians.

How to Stay Sane During Deployment:

1. Turn your broom closet into a palace by building your own loft! No seriously, you'd be amazed at what a bored soldier can do with time, lumber, and a saw.
2. Hit golf balls at the guys in the guard towers.
3. Get a pet! Stray dogs, cats, and scorpions make great ones! In one case I heard someone had swung a donkey...
4. Watch DVDs... A LOT of DVDs... Seriously, since I've been here I've gone through every movie I have twice, a ton of bootlegs, the entire series of Rome, Seasons 1-3 of Entourage, and I'm getting all of The Shield next.
5. Check your email.
6. Check your email again.
7. Clean your weapon.
8. Clean your weapon again.
9. Change your buddy's computer desktop to pictures of David Hasselhoff from Baywatch.
10. Rearrange your wall locker.
11. Sneak into your commander's office and take a picture of yourself mooning him while he sleeps.
11a. Not recommended to try this with your First Sergeant.
12. Eat care package candy.
13. Play X-Box.
14. Play your buddy's X-Box.
15. Play tag with incoming mortar rounds.
16. Write motivational phrases on outgoing mortar rounds and main gun rounds.

Yeah, I'm bored. Just like my dad said about police work, this job is hours upon hours of sheer boredom followed by seconds and minutes of heart pounding fear and excitement. Till Next time.

### Email: January 8, 2007 (Day 79)

Today I played "follow the trail of bodies and pools of blood." It started off when we rolled up by accident on a police truck that hit by an IED. Initial thought was it had got to hell in an ambush or drive by. There were that many holes in it. Blood on the seats inside. Blood in streaks down the doors. Blood pooled underneath the car. Blood running down the street in the rain.

Locked the area down and search the apartment behind it. Find collateral blast damage on the building, in the apartment... trying to talk to one lady and this other is in my ear and just won't shut the fuck up about how the stray shrapnel killed her fucking dog. Take pictures of everything and roll to the police station. Roll into the parking lot and see four police gathered around the back of their pickup truck messing with something under a bloody sheet. Move over to the truck and we see the victim of an "EJK" or "Extrajudicial Killing"... you know, one of the buzz words someone in the rear comes up with and gets a medal for. Guy's hands are bound behind his back, forehead is split open, and the back of his skull is missing.

We get to work. I hold the head up by the hair (a human head at dead weight is heavier than I thought) and get a picture of the half that's missing. Pull the shirt down, put my finger by the entry wound under the Adam's apple to give size perspective, and take a picture of that entry wound. Lift the shirt up and get pictures of the two shots to the side. Pull the eyelid open to photograph the blood pooling behind the eye. Squeeze the flesh to tell how fresh he is. Try to close his eyelids, but they keep sliding open into that same sickening look of shock, the look wondering what he did to get murdered like a dog in the street behind his house, the look I keep seeing every time I close my eyes, even to fucking blink. So I'm done here, having reduced this dentist with a wife, kids, family, career, and life down to a series of photos and notes for a fucking PowerPoint debrief for some intel analyst to plot on a board somewhere and some Colonel to peruse at his leisure over his morning coffee. Then we move to where it happened and sweep the area. It's amazing how much blood the rain will wash off the grass and the mud and down into the street. This guy definitely wasn't the only one dumped here.

And behind it all, the knowledge we're always two steps behind, one hour too late. Never getting a chance to meet these assholes in the act and gun them down in the street instead of finding this poor guy instead. It's not even like being a big city police officer. Special Operations forces here have tons more resources than the conventional army. Those guys here do hits left and right, they take down bad guys, find caches, they get something TANGIBLE. Back home, people call police when shots are fired in a neighborhood because people trust the police and the police can catch the bad guys, even if the revolving door of American courts puts them back out again. The local thug may beat you up if you call the police and he finds out. He may even kill you. He won't, most likely, kidnap you, torture you, cut off your head and stick it on the gate to your house, and leave your family's bodies shot in the ditch in front, or in a neat little pile in pieces on the floor of your living room, and paint a warning to your neighbors on your gate in your own blood. We always get there an hour too late, a day too late. We catch bad guys off of dumb luck or their own stupidity. What a day. And I still have 10 months left. Yay.

### Email: January 11, 2007 (Day 82)

Cause: Last night higher loosened ROE in Iraq to help bring the country, especially Baghdad, under control

Effect: Brigade launches sixty 155mm artillery shells into an area of Baghdad nine kilometers west of the FOB.

Reaction from soldiers: It's about damn time.

So yeah, I'm sitting here in my room working on the support form for my first evaluation when the explosions start. I don't mean one or two. I mean a lot. A whole lot. We're thinking "well, I guess JAM's mortar rounds are reaching the expiration date, and it's time to use or lose." In reality, we find out it's our brigade launching a 60 round artillery strike, and the sound of outgoing is music to our ears… especially since the President recently announced more troops and extensions for units here (there is a good chance I may be extended by up to four months).

We are trying to play catch-up against a powerful and well developed insurgency that not only holds the legitimacy of violence in most of Baghdad, but also holds a large chunk of LEGITIMATE political power. Could you imagine what America in the '20s and '30s would have been like if the mob controlled the Departments of Defense, Energy, Transportation and a large chunk of the Department of State? Well, just look at Iraq and there's your example.

Instead of crushing and killing Muqtada al-Sadar and his cronies 2 years ago when we had the chance (oops) we believed him when he said he wanted to "help us out" and "be part of the new Iraq." Now his militia is strong enough that a month ago it overran and held an Iraqi town south of Baghdad for a day. He was instrumental in getting several Iraqi politicians elected and the "Sadr Bureau" controls several key ministries, including power, and infiltrated the police so much that people are more afraid of the cops than the criminals. One way or another, will have to eliminate the militias in Baghdad before we can go home, and with more IRAQI troops coming to Baghdad and getting comfortable inflicting a higher level of violence, we may stand a chance.

### **Email: January 12, 2007 (Day 83)**

So last night's patrol got interesting. On our way out the gate, 3rd Platoon tanks hit an IED on the way to the checkpoint. No one hurt, just caught a trash bag on fire and cooked off a few rounds sitting in the bustle rack. I move my patrol to the blast site to take pictures of the blast and here's the scene I find: Traffic is backed up behind both tanks securing the site, and the site is in full view of several small buildings with no cover except for the vehicles behind us. Oh yeah, did I mention that this SAME spot was used for IEDs twice in the last week? Yeah, real cool. So after we make sure there are no other IEDs in the area, I get out with two guys to take pictures. I get to the blast crater, pull out my camera, and hear a burst of machine gun fire with a whiz-crack. The rest of the scene is best described by my lead truck commander:

"Hey sir, that was Blue shooting a warning shot at a car trying to roll on you. I was watching y'all, heard the shot, looked at them, and by the time I turned back 3 seconds later you somehow magic-ed yourself across 50 meters, opened the door, got in your truck, and shut it again"

Yeah, I've never moved so fast in my life. It's funny now, but it really wasn't at the time.

One other noteworthy incident: I got into my first legit car chase. Seriously, we were doing 40 down narrow crowded streets chasing a car. Unfortunately, we lost them when the street split three ways. Now let me tell you, up-armored HMMWVs are not the most maneuverable vehicles in the world. They weigh a couple tons and are notorious for rolling over. So yeah, doing 30 mph around tight turns feeling your vehicle leaning up was kind of hair raising... but it sure was a hell of a lot of fun. Not much else going on here. It's pouring outside and I hope it stops before I roll out tonight although it probably won't. I go on leave in a month. I can't wait to get out of here for a bit and see Sara. Until then, it's just doing what we do everyday: wake up, go on patrol, and try not to get shot or blown up

### Email: January 14, 2007 (Day 85)

Last night my platoon got hit again. It was another EFP, the same kind that destroyed my tank... except this time it hit my lead truck 50 meters in front of me. Luckily, the driver saw it and stopped short. As they crept forward to get a better look, they saw what it was and got on the radio... and the triggerman decided to cut his losses and blow it. The bomb shredded the front tire on the blast side, tore through the engine and destroyed it, and exited out the other side of the engine block. It missed the cab of the truck entirely and no one got hurt. We pulled forward to the next intersection, and all the anger, hate, and frustration boiled over. I was tired of this shit, and we were hitting back. I caught movement out the corner of my eye. I walked to the house and kicked the gate in. When it got stuck I bashed it down till it tore from the hinges. I grabbed the first guy out of the house and tossed him to the pavement. Next guy got the same. Men, boys, women, kids, emptied the whole thing and stuck them against the wall. I was going to clear the area and find this son of a bitch. Next house. I kicked the door so hard the frame splintered and the hinges broke. Emptied it out. Next house, same thing. We emptied four houses when we spotted the guy again. We fired, missed, and chased him on foot down a block. Kicked in the gate he went through. Shout for the occupants to come out. Father comes out and I snatched him by the collar and slammed him on the wall.

Where is he?

Mister, I don't know!

You didn't see anyone come in?

No, mister no!

You didn't hear anything just now?

No mister!

You're telling me you didn't hear that explosion 200 feet away from your house about five minutes ago?

No, mister, no!

I drag him towards the others we rounded up. We move to the upstairs door. It's locked from the inside. We try beating it down. No dice. We can't get in. I call it off and move back to our trucks. We hook everything up and get ready to move, and what does battalion want? Pictures. They want me to stay in the kill zone to take pictures. No matter we flushed the guy out, found his hide, and everyone is ok. All they care about are pictures of the blast site. After a long string of swearing over the radio, I snapped crappy ones and get us the hell out of there. No one in my platoon is worth a damn photograph.

Oh, and this all occurs AFTER our commander's "trusted" informant rolls us into an ambush. By the grace of God the guys at the site must have thought we were lost, so they just harassed us instead of killed us. I rolled four trucks and 12 guys into an insurgent compound based on the informant's word. I'm not kidding. It was by far the STUPIDEST thing I've ever done in my life. We rolled in and the whole place goes dark. Three minutes later, lights come up, and we're surrounded. The only exit is blocked off and we're being pushed in deeper. The crowd was about 100 openly hostile people, with about 30 guys with the perfect look of militia foot soldiers. My only thought was "If it comes down to it, I'm killing everybody to get out of here. Men, women, kids, anyone in the street in our way dies. WE are making it out alive. They let us go, and I mean that. THEY let US go. And my commander's first question when I got back? Did you get pictures?

No sir, I just came back with personnel counts, house descriptions, enemy actions on arrival, and a memorized layout that perfectly matches the satellite imagery you pulled up. But did you get pictures? So I lied. Yes sir, but they didn't turn out, it was dark. What I meant to say was, I didn't take any, you asshat, because one flash going off, one person sees us pulling out a camera, and this goes from "oh look, they're lost, let's mess with them" to "ok, they're up to something, kill them all." Like I said, no one in my platoon is worth a photograph when we can pull better images up from a satellite, and if that makes me a bad platoon leader, then my commander can kiss my ass.

## Email: January 15, 2007 (Day 86)

What's shown on TV is not reality. The news clips, even the "combat clips" are sanitized sound bites for TV. They show the soldier kicking in the door (like last week on CNN), but they don't show what happens next: noise, smoke, confusion, gunshots, guy ducked round the corner, go after him, room clear, check the- GUN GUN GUN!!!! One, two, 15 shots fired, check the next- BEHIND YOU! BANG! Did he have a weapon? I don't know? DID HE HAVE A WEAPON? SERGEANT, I DON'T KNOW! I DON'T KNOW! IT WAS ALL SO FAST! Holy shit, he's just a kid....

Congratulations, 18 year old Johnny from Ohio, you got your first kill... on a 14 year old boy who jumped out a door to your right, or on a kid holding a toy pistol, or on the woman who ran into the hallway right in front of you. Here's your combat patch, combat action badge, and some Trazodone to help you sleep for the next year of your life. Who's to blame? Whose fault is it? Is Johnny a criminal? Why didn't he know it was a civilian? Why didn't he take the time to make sure?

I'll tell you why. If Johnny is clearing a house full of armed men (and being the brave men insurgents are, they love to fight around women and children), and is fighting his way room to room, that extra second he takes may not kill him... it'll kill his buddy, and THAT is one thing a soldier cannot bare to live with. Accidently killing an innocent in a combat situation is one thing, but letting your buddy get hurt or killed is utterly unbearable. The first thing you learn in the Army, on day one, is you ARE your brother's keeper. You see a kid with a gun pointing at your guys, then you don't look twice to see if it's a toy, you shoot. If you do not believe that a child is capable of murder, then you haven't been paying attention, even in our own country.

You are your brother's keeper.

Fight or flight. It's a simple choice. Binary. Black or white. Yes or no. The ultimate instinct self-preservation, and only the most admirable human traits override it: love, duty, self-sacrifice, and courage. What I wrote to you yesterday is the part that isn't on the news. Were those people innocent? Yes. Did I care? No. Was I willing to tear the block apart to find the guy? Yes. Was it justified? Yes. Was it the right thing to do? Yes.

Insurgency, while political, acts like an infection, like a virus. It infests, infects, and multiplies, until it chokes off the rest of the healthy system. The violence is the symptom. However, FEW insurgencies remain true to their political roots, because power has a way of corrupting human beings. I highly doubt Muqtada al-Sadr, the leader of the Mahdi Militia here in Iraq, only has an hour of power a day, no clean water, and is living in the same slum the majority of Iraqis are. What we have in Iraq began as every other insurgency, and has devolved into what most become: organized thuggery. Even the Taliban, for all of its Muslim Puritanism, thrived and financed itself off of the Opium trade in Afghanistan. I'm sure that's allowed in the Koran somewhere. Eventually, most insurgencies end up accomplishing none of its STATED political goals, but it has accomplished the main one: handing over the reins of wealth and power to someone else. The rest is rhetoric.

However, the root of the problem at our level is not political and social unrest: it's fear. Why didn't the man I dragged down the street tell me what I know he knew? Simple: he feared the militia more than he feared me. I may hit him, I may drag him down the block, I may even take him to jail, but I WON'T come for him in the middle of the night to torture and kill his family and make him watch before I kill him. I WON'T bind his hands and shoot him in the street like a dog and leave his body as a warning. Without removing fear you cannot treat the disease. You can't rebuild infrastructure when you can't provide security, you can't establish security when you can't find the bad guys, you can't find the bad guys when people won't tell you where they are, and people won't tell you where they are when they're afraid of being killed for it. Remove the fear, and the rest flows.

If you follow the logic, then you see the inherent problem. Find the bad guys to remove the fear so you can find the bad guys. This process is not linear; it is a linear path stemming from a conditional loop. The largest mistake was skipping to the last step before we finished the first. THAT is why we are still here. Like the medic says, kill the enemy, THEN treat your buddy. We didn't kill the enemy, and we're trying to treat our buddy while he's still being shot. We patch one hole and another opens.

### **Email: January 23, 2007 (Day 94)**

So it's been a while since my last letter. I've been busy... real busy. In a short synopsis: car chases, foot chases, finding homicides, IEDs, bombings on civilians, and firing my first shots with intent. Let me tell you, nothing caps off a night like chasing a guy through an open garbage/sewage field into an animal market, while you slosh through God knows what and pools of blood you pray are from an animal (let's just say it was behind the site of the murders, and I wasn't too keen about having to sanitize my boots with bleach). We're looking to transition to a different sector in a week or two. Good news: more bad guys and more probability to make arrests that will stick. Bad news: more bad guys. We'll have to see what happens. Next month I go on leave and get to spend a couple of weeks relaxing and spending time with Sara. I won't have anything other than a disposable, pre-paid cell phone, but I'll get the number out. Thank you all again for all the love and support, and I'll write more soon.

### Email: January 27, 2007 (Day 98)

So, we think that the bad guys got resupplied as they are shelling and bombing the shit out of us. Mortar fire for three days straight, with a break yesterday (Friday is their Sunday), so we figure it will resume tonight. Two days ago, one mortar hit our barracks. It went into the building that houses our 1st and Headquarters platoons. It dropped right through the roof of one room and detonated inside, destroying the room and damaging two others. Luckily, the guys who lived there were out on patrol and no one was hurt. We're just waiting for it to calm down again... I'm just waiting for leave. I've stopped watching CNN and reading the news for the most part, as all it does these days is annoy me. Other than that, not much is going on over here. I took the graveyard shift for the next couple of weeks as it lets me talk to Sara in the evenings, so I spend the time reading books and writing. Oh, and we might get crammed back on top of each other with the $82^{nd}$ is coming to our FOB. We're only done with a quarter of deployment and we're all still waiting for the news of our extension (I've already mentally prepared myself for the possibility of an extra four months here). It will probably be slow for awhile, but that's fine with me. Better to be bored than having bullets winging by my head and bombs going off on my tank.

### Email: February 8, 2007 (Day 110)

White 3: White 1, White 3, we think we spotted the guys just around- CONTACT DISMOUNTS! WHITE 1, WE'RE TAKING FIRE ON OUR DISMOUNTS!

Me: White 6A, White 1, hey, what's going on down there, anyone hurt?

White 6A: White 1, 6A, I don't know, we're taking fire and OH SHIT! HANSON! HANSON! MEDI- (static).

Me: White 6, White 1, SITREP! (static) White 6A, this is White 1, somebody talk to me down there.

White 6A: 1, this is 6A, Hanson's ok, he just fell. Continuing pursuit.

White 3: White 1, White 3, suppressing target. HEY! GET BACK BEHIND THE BRADLEY, DAMMIT! HE'S BEHIND THAT WALL. White 1, White 3, I got him behind a low wall.

Me: White 3, White 1, smoke him. Level that wall and splatter his ass all across the street! (Firing from a chain gun)

White 3: White 1, White 3, Hell yeah! We have one confirmed enemy KIA. Continuing pursuit.

Me: White 3, White 1, roger, understand one enemy KIA. Continue pursuit and kill the second RPG gunner. Let's see if we can get two on the board tonight.

White 3: White 1 negative, he ducked over a berm and I'll have to give him a belly shot on the Bradley to continue.

Me: White 3, White 1, roger, halt pursuit, consolidate on the objective, and clear the body.

White 3: White 1, White 3, roger, understood, although it may not take too long, sir, there wasn't much left of him after I hit him with HE.

Me: This is White 1, Roger. Good job. Let's clear him and get out of here.

That was a truncated version of the radio traffic on my platoon net last night. What started as a normal patrol turned into my platoon ambushing the ambushers, hunting them down through neighborhood streets, killing one, and wounding another who later surrendered to another American unit. That night, with two or three short transmissions I turned a quiet neighborhood into a battleground, with small arms and high explosive rounds from a 25mm chain gun flying down the streets, smashing through walls, into cars, and into the enemy. Last night, from 200m away sitting in my tank guarding against another ambush I ordered the death of a human being. After it was all over, there was joy, elation, feelings of success and vindication, a feeling of "yes, tonight we hit back and we hit back harder." When that passed all I felt was a kind of numbness.

We killed the enemy, but it wasn't the enemy we expected. It wasn't the hardcore jihadist who bled the Koran and fought against us as another soldier. No, it was a guy who got $40, two days wage for an Iraqi, to take a rocket launcher and a rifle with his buddy and try to assault an American patrol. The only choice he had was, most likely, to take the money, do the attack, and hope to live… or to turn it down and be killed by the militia. It's sad and depressing. I ordered the death of a man who probably didn't have a choice in the matter. He'd almost certainly been lied to about the capabilities of our armor, who didn't realize the suicidal nature of attacking U.S. tanks and Bradleys with only two men, one anti-personnel rocket, and

48

one rifle, of attacking a convoy which, by itself, could pulverize the whole block and then some.

Last night I was surrounded by grins and congratulations from my Soldiers, the infantry guys, and my bosses. We had killed the enemy, and I was happy. I was happy we got the bad guys, that we made them pay, that I could command men under fire, and that we accomplished the mission while taking no casualties. But when I called Sara later that night it all just seemed so hollow. No guilt, they were clearly insurgents and would have killed us if we hadn't killed them. No joy either. We had killed a couple of poor guys trying to make a buck. So what then? I don't know. Maybe I'll figure it out. Hopefully, I won't have to do this again. But if I do, I'll do it in a heart beat, with every weapon I have, with enough fire power to level the whole street, because, the only thing that matters, truly matters, is bringing us all home in one piece.

## **Email: February 11, 2007 (Day 113)**

So, just finished the first week in the new sector, and here's my impression. Imagine if the Bronx, Watts, and Compton got drunk and had an illegitimate love child. That's Kamaliyah and Fedilayah. My favorite has been the roving gang of rock launching children, who are pretty good at tagging the small part of your head sticking out of your hatch while your tank is rolling.... from almost 50 ft away. I'm serious, they're like little artillery pieces with those things. I'm not saying this place is unfriendly. Oh no, we've moved far past unfriendly. Openly hostile and violent is a better word. Kids and teenagers sneering, spitting on the tank, and throwing things. The stereotypical military age males eyeing you hard as you eye them back.

We even had one guy who was stupid enough to make the "throat-cutting" gesture towards me. Don't think he'll ever do it again. He didn't look to happy after my infantrymen had a chat with him. This place is the Wild West... if the Wild West was hopped up on PCP and given tank-killing bombs and automatic weapons.

Seriously, I can't even describe it. It defies any rational explanation. In one week my Company has killed a guy who tried to ambush us (me), hit an IED and found another (Red Platoon), been shot at who knows how many times (EVERYBODY), and numerous other small encounters of "who's the biggest dog in the yard" (i.e. throat-cutter guy). That's the game every day: who's the biggest dog in the yard? They throw rocks, we throw them back. They throw more, we zip shots over their heads. They hit us, we hit back harder. It's like a bad cop show.

More than anything, it gets tiresome. I am tired of pointing my pistol at people, I am tired of throwing smoke grenades to scatter crowds of child thugs, and I am tired of the constant power games. Look too soft, and you get hit. That's the end all be all. And in the middle of it all, are the people who get caught in the middle... like the little two year old girl I played peek-a-boo with from my tank hatch who giggled and clapped and waved at me. It's amazing what transcends cultural and language barriers: smiles, waves, a gun in the face, a hard look from a hard man. It's amazing what effects are produced when you're staring down the barrel of a loaded gun, and that's on both sides of the coin, not just us doing it to them. Ha, us and them. That's really what it boils down: Us versus them. Us versus Them with the little girls caught in the crossfire.

The worst thing is, when you earn your living dealing with the dregs of humanity every day you start thinking every one is like that. It makes me sad. There are good people here, but they're out numbered by the scum, by the dregs, by the people who may not be criminals but are just as guilty for turning a blind eye or letting it happen. Sure, they're just trying to survive in all this, it's either help the bad guys or wind up in a ditch with two in the head for some LT to find and process, but when does enough become enough? When does any of this become enough? We're making progress here, we're pushing the enemy back, and we've got them on the run... or so the briefs say. Yeah, it's quieted down since we took over, but I roll out and see the same thing every day and nothing's changed. A few people still smile at me, many glare at me, and even more want me dead, with a handful stupid enough to try. I see the same thing, day in, day out, and at the end of each day there is only one thing on my mind: one more day down, one more day of life at the close, and one more day I brought them all back. Nothing like the words "CONTACT! White 1, I'm taking fire!" to make your blood run cold, and nothing like the words "Roger, confirmed enemy KIA" to put it all back at ease. It's such a weird existence. It's like waking up in something that is so bizarre your mind starts to convince itself that none of it is real. You're only living out a movie. All I want to do is see the credits roll and go home.

### **Email: February 26, 2007 (Day 128)**

So here I sit, in a hotel room at Disney World, ending my first week of leave, and I have some very astute observations to make:

1. The States do not smell.
2. I CAN drink the water from the faucet.
3. The first 100 feet or so of the horizon is blue, not a dingy shade of brownish-yellow.

4. The loud bangs, crashes, and booms ARE just slamming doors/back firing cars/the TV.
5. No one is trying to kill me.

    I had forgotten how different the world is back here. How much you take for granted. Speaking of a different world, Sara and I got to spend a couple days together at her FOB, Victory Base Complex (VBC) before flying out to the States. The biggest thing to know about Victory is that it used to be used by Saddam and friends as a private resort. The next biggest thing that struck me about Victory was that it really was inside the wire in the truest sense... as in no one was trying to kill me when I was on the FOB. Seriously, aside from the rare mortar attack you might as well be back on a post in the States. They even have traffic cops (no joke, Sara got a ticket on her bike for forgetting her reflective belt at the office). I remember hearing a controlled detonation go off (the engineers blow up munitions that are found) and the first thing I do is bolt for the trailer door while Sara sat there looking at me wondering what the heck I was doing.

    You never really know how much a situation has affected you until you're no longer neck deep in it, until you're no longer looking over your shoulder, until your mind finally registers "Hey, relax, no one is trying to kill you." You get a massive outpouring of tension... followed by relief... and then followed by guilt. Finally, the strangest thing of all: you start to miss it. You find you feel more awkward back in this alternate reality than in your "normal" world, and you wonder what that means. You find things start to itch just under the surface. You miss the rumble of the track beneath your feet, the burning smell of gunpowder and cordite, and the throb of the pack. You find it all seems a little out of place back here.

I still have a week of leave left and I realized something: It would have been easier to never have left at all than to taste life again for two weeks merely to lose it for another eight months. I'm eternally thankful for the time I have now and the time I get to spend with Sara, but I know what waits for me. Honestly, I don't know what bugs me more: that I HAVE to go back or that part of me WANTS to go back, because for the life of me I can't get this to feel normal...

# Part II:
# Downhill Slide

*Mid-tour leave was amazing. Sara and I spent it in Disney World down in Florida and in Atlanta visiting my family. Still, it felt like an alternate reality. No gear, no weapons, no explosions, just clean air, indoor plumbing, beer, and each other. I spent so much of my leave trying to savor every moment, every kiss, and every shred of happiness to carry me until October when I came home. However, despite leave being great, the first cracks were showing.*

*I lost count of how many times I jumped at loud noises. One night I went from a dead sleep to trying to crawl under the bed due to a loud noise in the hotel parking lot. I kept seeing the dead's faces, tortured Iraqis we would find on patrol, people we killed, and everyday victims of random violence. Crowds made me anxious. I couldn't relax unless my back was to a wall with clear sight lines on the exits. Whenever I looked at children I kept seeing the little girl killed in a market bombing.*

*I ignored all of it: the uneasiness, the hyperawareness, and the flashbacks, all of it. I hadn't been in combat that long. I hadn't seen anything too horrible. Everybody else was fine. I must be weak at some level. Too top it off, I was an Officer. I needed to suck it up and drive on. These feelings and behaviors were nothing to worry about, right? Wrong. These were the first indicators a deeper issue was forming. I should have examined what was happening to me instead of brushing it off. I should have started talking to people then. Instead, I ignored it, determined to drive on and complete the mission like a good soldier.*

*Despite those early indicators leave was a happy time. Sara had six months left and I had nine. Despite contact in our sector, there had been nothing truly horrible or earth shattering. I could do this pace for another nine months, no sweat. I was comfortable as a platoon leader and leading in combat. I knew my sector, I knew my Soldiers, and I felt confident in my abilities. Nine more months and it was back into Sara's arms and, if everything went right, she'd be my fiancée soon after.*

*And then my world started falling apart.*

### Email: March 11, 2007 (Day 141)

So, I got a little surprise when I got back to Iraq. While waiting at BIAP (Baghdad International Airport... and by "airport" I mean a flight line, runway, a few tents, and a concrete pad where you sit and wait for your bird) I ran into one soldier from the other tank company in our battalion. I wave to him, and he greets me with "Hey sir, how's it feel to be an XO?" I sat there and stared at him for a second, figuring that he was confused. I was a Platoon Leader in Charlie, not the Delta Executive Officer. Well, after a few calls to my Company I finally got word. Not rumor or word of mouth, but official. I wasn't a Platoon Leader anymore. I got bumped up to XO and moved to Delta along with a new Commander.

Part of me was happy, really happy. Yes, someone finally recognized my efforts, yes, I got a job promotion, and yes, I had a new challenge... Still, a bigger part of me was a little disappointed, and kind of hurt. I wasn't a PL anymore, and, even worse, I had heard about it through word of mouth that the switch had happened... while I was gone. No real chance to say goodbye to my guys and, worst of all, no last ride, no last patrol, no last chance to savor being a Platoon Leader. Yeah, I'll roll as an XO, but it isn't the same. The guys on the patrol aren't YOURS the way they are when you're a Platoon Leader. I have to take care of a company now, not just my platoon. This should be fun. Is it bad I need a beer already and I've only been back two days?


### Email: March 20, 2007 (Day 150)

Since I returned from leave Baghdad has exploded.

"Four dead, two wounded in roadside bomb attack in East Baghdad" runs on the CNN News ticker.

You mean Heath and the others who died that day. Not to mention Gray, who died in a hospital bed in Germany after multiple surgeries, an amputation, and his 1SG just getting off the phone with his wife saying he'll be ok. You mean the PL, my classmate, who was in his first week on the job and just lost four NCOs and one more Soldier right when he took over. You mean four widows and three orphans. You mean five brothers.

SIGACT: IED strike on Cobra White 3. Three minor casualties. A Bradley burning to the ground while the ammo cooks off inside... while Battalion asks the guys, MY guys, to "get closer and determine what hit it." I'll give you a hint: it left a three and a half foot deep crater and it went boom.

SIGACT: IED strike on Desperado White 3. My second day in the company and I'm flying to get recovery assets pushed out to get it back. No casualties. Tank destroyed.

Seven days. Five dead. Four wounded. Two vehicles destroyed. My Battalion straining to keep itself balanced.

Every day is a struggle, a struggle between the baser instincts and morality, between revenge and ethics, between savagery and restraint. We talk of heroes, we talk of sacrifice. Presidents and Generals, Colonels and Sergeants Major, and Commanders far and wide espouse the Army values, talk of courage and sacrifice, bravery, loyalty... They come to memorials with salutes and bowed heads while flashbulbs go off, while the Soldiers and his family wait "for the official party to depart" so they can come forward to pay their respects. You know who the hero is? It isn't just the man who sacrificed his life doing his duty to his country. It's also the young 19 year old Private who gets back in his gear, into his truck, and rolls back out the wire the next day, dry eyed and stoned faced because the best way to honor the memory of the fallen is to get back on the horse and ride out again. It is the platoon leader, squad leader, and team leader who have men with hate in their hearts and murder in their eyes waiting for the word... but says stand down instead. It is the men who pick each other up, wipe each other's eyes, and hold the family together. Those are heroes, and ones we often forget.

## **Email: March 30, 2007 (Day 160)**

I've been busy the last couple of weeks. I guess that's the joy of being an XO. Still, with all the paperwork I'm loaded down with, I still manage to sneak out the wire for a patrol every now and again so I don't get cabin fever too bad.

Life right now is either incredibly busy or not busy at all. In fact, once I get done with a couple things in a couple days my daily workload will drop to damn near zero... which will be nice... sort of. At least then I'll be able to go on patrol more. No word of getting extended yet, but another brigade in 2ID got extension orders. It's kind of tricky for my Battalion: We belong to The Cav, but we're attached to 2ID, so we have no idea where the extension will come from if it does and which will apply to us. 3ID just got here, and I talked to some of their guys. Their orders say 18 months. That's right. They have orders to deploy for a year and a half. Oh yeah, and they were just here eight months ago… and we wonder why we can't retain people in the Army.

You can only work 14 to 16 hour days every day for so long before you cease to be effective. I've gone out the wire so tired that I would blink and lose 20-30 minutes of time at a stretch. Yeah, I was really combat effective then. Oh on top of the 18 months away from home they'll be manning "combat outposts" which comprise the following: find abandoned building (in my old company's case it turned out to be a half burned potato chip factory), occupy abandoned building, stay there for five days at a stretch, come back to FOB for one day, spend one day back doing maintenance, drop off laundry, get a phone call in (maybe), check internet (if it works), sleep (if you can because you're trying to cram everything else in), and then go back out for another five days. Three of the companies in my Battalion have been doing it for about two months and they're all beat. Morale is dropping fast.

On top of all of that, we just found out most of the MREs we shipped to the outposts (including our JSS) are bad. I don't mean slightly spoiled. I mean rotten. I guess that's what happens when you leave food here for three years in temperatures from 40 to 120 over the year and never replace them. Seriously, moldy food and guys getting sick bad. Way to go Surge. Oh yeah, and on top of it all we're getting shot up and blown up. But at least we're knocking down targets. Care packages always welcome, especially the little things of mandarin oranges. I'm addicted to those things. The last package of the little orange cups I got I ate them all in a day.

### Email: April 4, 2007 (Day 165)

On Monday, I found out that a friend and classmate of mine, Neale Shank, died of wounds while over here in Iraq. I still don't know the details. Yesterday, my company was in contact three times over the course of the day. The first resulted in the death of PFC Gabriel Figaroa, a 20 year old medic, killed by a sniper. The night's last were IED strikes on two Bradleys. Both caught fire. The first Bradley burned to the ground and wounded one of the crew. The company is spent, physically and emotionally. Some guys logged 20 hours in sector. The platoon who lost their medic wasn't supposed to roll till today, but when the Brads went down last night they saddled up and rolled out again. I woke up that morning and had told my 1SG that I was going to take a couple hours to myself and get my head straight after finding about Neale. 10 minutes into that time I was talking to Sara and got the initial report.

"Sir, you better come quick. Red's in contact, taking fire, and they're trying to break contact to get Fig to Loyalty. He's hurt pretty bad."

And so began the spiral. Talking into two radios and a telephone, coordinating air and ground assets, screaming at BN to quit bothering my commander with trivia while he's hitting houses, and praying to God that the guys out on the ground don't lose any more people and kill anyone innocent... and hoping they do find the guy who killed Fig and tear him apart. Then, when it was all said and done, we sent a relief out for our White platoon so they could be there when we loaded Fig's body on the bird to send him home.... and they got hit coming in. Same thing: elevated sniper fire. Thankfully, the shots came late as they mounted up to leave... and they turned and melted the barrels on their guns, ripping buildings and rooftops apart. Then, when we thought it was done for the day, the scouts went on their patrol and had a Bradley blown up. As the other Bradley rushed to help, it hit a secondary IED. Brad burning, rounds cooking off, more wounded, and the company rode out in force, with Fig's platoon thundering down the MSR in tanks bringing recovery assets with them, locked, loaded, and looking for someone to kill. It was a day packed with pain, violence, and trauma... and they did everything right.

That's the hardest thing to handle. You do everything right, and people still die. Then there's the questioning. Why did we do this? Why didn't we do that? I was five feet away from him. Why didn't the sniper shoot me instead? What more could I have done? Why was I back here and not in the fight? Although 1SG assured me that I was doing my job here, and doing it impressively, it wasn't enough for me. I wanted to be out there just like everyone else, taking the same risk as everyone else. The stress crashed down on me last night. I was done. I sat outside the CP smoking God knows what cigarette of the day and I shook from complete exhaustion. Then, I couldn't sleep. I spent the night tossing and turning, mind restless.

And today, I got up and did my job. I laughed, I joked, I walked dry eyed and steady voiced. I got up today with that burning coal of anger, sadness, and hatred smoldering and using it to carry me one step after the other. Yeah, it hurts, yes, it will for a while, and yes all I want to do is rip that neighborhood apart and find the son of a bitch who killed our boy. This is what the six o'clock doesn't show you. We still have a long way to go, especially if we get extended, but each day we lean on each other a little more, cover down a little tighter, and put one foot in front of the other. It isn't for the mission, it isn't for God and Country, it's for each other, the way soldiers have always fought.

...And our hearts are standing attention,
While we wait for their passing tread...

# Part III:
# Blood

*Few things affected me on this deployment like Neale's death. Neale was a huge part of why I joined the Army. I first met him in my high school's JROTC program. I remember watching him with all the wide eyed wonder a 14 year old freshman could muster. He was confident, athletic, strong, smooth, and utterly, completely sure of himself. To me he was larger than life.*

*Neale encouraged me to become active in JROTC. I joined the drill teams because of Neale. I went to summer camps because of Neale. I did the camping, volunteer work, and everything connected to the program because of Neale. Neale graduated two years ahead of me and enlisted, and at that point I began seriously considering the Army. Instead of enlisting I pursued West Point. However, in a pleasant surprise, I learned that Neale had done the same, applying to the Prep School and getting accepted. Neale and I would be classmates.*

*Four years of suck and many a shared plane ride home later, we'd both graduate, with Neale commissioning as an Infantryman while I chose Armor. We went our separate ways and didn't see each other for a while. When I least expected it, I ran into Neale in a bar while home on leave. He would deploy soon, so we did what any two soldiers did in that situation: drank copiously. As we got ready to leave, we said we'd get together again one last time. Once again, the usual happened: life got in the way, schedules didn't line up, I missed a call, he forgets to return another, and so on, and so on. I never saw Neale again.*

*He was my friend and I couldn't make the fucking time and the next thing I hear, while halfway around the world trying not to drown in the violent shithole of East Baghdad, is that he's dead. I hear it with a half lit, knock off Camel dangling from my lip, a finger in one ear, and a cheap, piece of shit, Iraqna cell phone pressed to the other. I hear it through the broken static as my mom keeps repeating it over and over, not sure if I heard her.*

*Neale's dead.*

*Neale's dead, Terron.*

*Hello?*

*Did you hear me?*

*Neale's dead.*

*And then Fig was killed.*

*Baghdad erupted into a full blown madhouse. Every day, someone took contact. It wasn't unusual for a battalion to have contact multiple times in a day. Hell, it wasn't unusual for a single company to have contact multiple times in a day. The violence escalated by the day, and it wasn't just us and the insurgents. Sectarian violence was spilling out of control. Civilians butchered by various Shia and Sunni insurgent groups. It wasn't uncommon for the insurgent groups to slug it out with each other. It was utter chaos. It was hell.*

*I'd become personally acquainted with death. Neale died. Fig died. Rustamiyah turned into a slaughterhouse. A patrol pulling up next to the hospital with a burned, shot up, or blown up vehicle became a regular occurrence. The curb by the hospital and flight line swam in blood. People on Rusty dying or gravely wounded on a regular basis. Rocket and mortar attacks happened often. Every day you woke up on Rustamiyah, even without going on patrol, could be the day you died.*

*Adding to all this, we would find out about the extension the worst possible way: from the news. The decision got leaked before anyone told the Army's rank and file. Families and soldiers everywhere got caught unaware. To make it even worse, the extensions were part of The Surge, no one knew if it included us as we deployed before The Surge began. We may be home in October as planned, or we could be here up to six months longer. None of us had any clear picture of what was happening.*

*I was in a constant state of stress. Guilt built up over Neale that I hadn't made more effort to see him one last time. I felt constantly behind the ever growing tide of work it took to keep our Company in the fight, especially with the pounding our Soldiers, vehicles, and equipment were taking. I was always angry and occasionally found it hard to contain myself. I didn't have a steady sleep cycle and my nicotine and caffeine consumption fell way above healthy limits.*

*Once again I ignored the warning signs. To make matters worse, we ignored them in each other. EVERYONE was pissed off. EVERYONE was tired. EVERYONE was stressed out. What made me different? The only guys who went to visit Combat Stress were the ones already known to be the slackers and the duds. They knew that if all else failed they could tell Combat Stress they were crazy and get a one-way ticket home or to the Green Zone for a few days. They were the soldiers trying any way possible to get out of the deployment and it was obvious. No one, even if you had legitimate problems, wanted to be lumped in with the shit bags, so no one went. We ignored the trained mental health professionals on our FOB because of perception issues. We all saw our fellow soldiers struggling right next to us, but no one wanted to acknowledge it. No one wanted to be the pussy who couldn't keep up while everyone else stayed in the fight.*

*Bodies were piling up on all sides, the fighting got fiercer, and we had no idea when it would all end. Our world became very narrow: find the enemy, kill the enemy, and survive this whole fucking mess. Unfortunately, just surviving became harder and harder to do.*

*Rustamiyah was drowning in blood.*

*It was the first time during the deployment that I became sure I was going to die.*

## Journal: April 13, 2007 (Day 174)

A lot of people have died this last week. We lost another from my Battalion the other day. A bomb cut right through the side of the truck and killed the guy riding shotgun and wounded two others. Since Neale died last Monday, eight more people in our AO have died, including three from my Battalion. Two days ago, I learned that another of my classmates was killed in Balad after he took a grenade to the back. We've been on commo blackout for nearly a week now. So, imagine Sara's worry when she happens to scroll through incident reports and sees one dead, three wounded from my Battalion, sees my unit mentioned in the incident, and hasn't heard a word from me in days. She didn't know we were not the ones hit. We were first responders, and I rolled out with the recovery to get the blown up vehicle. To top it all off, we found out about our extension yesterday.

To be more accurate, WE didn't find out about the extension, the families BACK HOME found out about the extension. Thank you for that one CNN. Imagine the emotions of Soldiers here at Rusty when they finally call home after a week only to be greeted with "Why didn't you tell us you were being extended!" and respond with "What extension?" Not only do you get extended, you have no time to prepare yourself or your family for it, and worst of all, you find out over chow while CNN plays on TV.

I've accepted it all with a dull resignation. The soul crushing weight of being here for three more months, of having to stay alive for three extra months, of wondering who will die and who'd be alive if it wasn't for the extension, still hasn't registered yet. I'm tired, and I want to go home.

### Email: April 14, 2007 (Day 175)

A full combat load of main gun ammunition for a tank is 42 rounds. Each rack in the turret holds 18 and six are held in the hull ammo storage that sits underneath the turret. Main gun rounds comprise the actual round and the casing. The casing for the main gun rounds is combustible, meaning that when the primer is hit by the firing pin, the entire round explodes, propelling the projectile. In short, pull trigger, round goes boom, and instead of a huge brass shell casing, all you're left with is the base cap and a tube sticking out of it that held the initial charge used to ignite the propellant. So yeah, they're sort of fragile, because if something penetrates the round it can set the thing off. That's why they're all tucked away behind blast doors, safety measures, and shit loads of armor.

The hull ammo storage holds six rounds. It's pretty much the last ditch emergency ammo in case you run out from the racks. It is designed so that it can be accessed from inside the turret by the crew remaining protected from enemy fire. Let that sink in. Six, highly explosive rounds of ammunition sit right under my crew's collective asses.

There are a lot of main gun rounds over here. Our company has so many every tank has full racks and plenty to spare. Tankers usually leave the hull storage empty unless they HAVE to put rounds in it (mostly because you forget they're there). There's a standing order to ensure the hull ammo storage is empty, but, like I said, occasionally people forget a round may be down there and not everything gets checked like it should. There's been plenty of times where we've stripped tanks for shipment to depot and found ammo in the hull ammo storage. The tank I was on today had been checked and, thankfully, the hull ammo storage was empty.

If rounds had been in the hull ammo storage today, then they would have ignited and exploded up from directly under my seat when the RPG hit my tank and drilled through the hull ammo storage. First time, the bomb just missed the fuel cell on my tank by six inches. This time, ammo that could have been in the hull storage wasn't there. Seven of Nine lives left. Nine months of deployment to go.

P.S. We're all ok and unhurt. Please say a prayer for PFC Trombles. He got shot in the arm today by a sniper. The bullet struck his back plate, rode along it, and hit his arm. He's lucky to be alive and was evacuated to Germany for surgery. I was locking down a road while the Company searched for the shooter. Tank got hit, Soldier got shot, it was a long ass day, but everyone's alive, and that's all that matters.

## Email: April 18, 2007 (Day 179)

When I first got over here, Anbar was the deadliest place to be in Iraq. I used to have a running joke I told whenever we were really getting into the suck: "Hey guys it could be worse, we could be in Anbar." Well, it looks like the Anbar guys are now saying "Hey guys, it could be worse, we could be in East Baghdad." Stars and Stripes reported today that Baghdad has officially become the most dangerous region in Iraq... and anyone in Baghdad will tell you, the places you don't want to be are the Peninsula, Market St., and 9 Nissan. Well, as luck would have it, we run 9 Nissan! Yay! To give you a clear picture, let me put it this way: If you're in the northwestern part of our Battalion's sector and you make a wrong turn you're in Sadr City. Yeah, we're the guys running along the Cambodian border chasing the new school Ho Chi Min Trail.

As we went over this kind of stuff in the XO meeting, some other things came to light. My Battalion has several other "records" in our possession:

-Most killed in action during a 30 day period since the start of the war: We lost nine in 30 days, with six being in one attack. This was reported in the Washington Post today with no prior warning to our Battalion... so the families got to read this one in the headlines. Thank you Washington Post. Hope you assholes sell a lot of papers. Go fuck yourselves.

-Largest and longest mortar barrage on a FOB. It was back in November, it lasted about six minutes, and they dropped 30 or 40 odd rounds, with most of them being in the last 30 seconds. It was one of the first times over here I was convinced I would die.

-And the one today, having ownership of the most dangerous area in Baghdad during one of the highest sustained periods of American deaths during the start of the war.

At this point, I'm pretty much numb, to tell you the truth. I just have to put one foot in front of the other for nine months and four days, and I'll be fine...

## Journal: April 28, 2007 (Day 189)

It's been a while since I've actually written just for myself, for me and no one else. Most of this experience has been recorded in the emails to the friends and family as a record of my thoughts and feelings, since I usually put the private thoughts in those... but sometimes, you need to write just for you, to say the things you can't tell anyone else.

I'm so angry. I don't know. I'm angry all the time. I wasn't even this angry as a PL.

Maybe it's the level of death and violence of the past few weeks. I saw Neale in the coffee shop the other day. While I was paying, I turned and staring right back at me was Neale, in the flesh, ACUs, haircut, with the same look in his eyes he always had. When I looked again in shock, it was somebody else, a guy who sort of looked like Neale, giving me an odd look in exchange for the crazy one I was giving him.

Maybe it's the stress and the workload. Maybe it's having no time to myself, just me. Maybe it's how I always snap at Sara when I don't mean to. Maybe it's the way I've felt this growing isolation ever since the extension was announced. Maybe it's a lot of things. Maybe it's nothing. One thing is clear, every day I wake up I feel like I'm coming closer and closer to losing my mind.

I don't know what to do to stop it, to stop all the hate and anger and rage that run through my heart everyday. This isn't healthy, and I know I'm not functioning the way I should. I can feel my mind slipping. I can feel my soul twisting into something black and cold and unrecognizable. I've lost who I am and I can't figure out how to get it back. Separating yourself doesn't work. There is no "leaving me in a box" while I go outside the wire. There's no shielding the inner parts of me from the horror and the pain of war. I want to scream.

The other night I cried myself to sleep. I screamed into my pillow. Then, I got out of bed, walked to my holster, put my pistol to my head, and pulled the trigger. I never told anyone. While it wasn't loaded, the psychological impact of putting my gun to my head, safety off, and pulling the trigger was heavy. It was a simple declaration: Help me. Help me, I can't do this anymore. I'm crazy, I've lost it, and I can't drown it out.

The depression hits me in full force and I don't have the strength left to fight it off anymore. Part of me wishes I had loaded the gun, and then it'd all have been over and done with. So quick, so easy. No more pain. No more loneliness. No more isolation. No more desert. No more death. No more friends dying. No more memorial services. No more saluting as the body of another one of our boys passes by towards the bird to be sent home. No more folded flags. No more empty bunks. No more, no more, no more. I want to go home. I want to go home. I want to go home.

### Email: May 16, 2007 (Day 207)

SSG Harper's memorial service got held up for a week. Not because of operations, or attacks, or anything else. It was because the "VIPs" couldn't attend. It was because the "VIPs" didn't have enough time to arrange transport. It was because the Colonels and Sergeants Major and Brigade and Battalion Commanders couldn't make it. It was because brass that never knew the Soldier, his life, or his family, would miss the photo op of having their pictures taken dropping their coin at the foot of a photograph, touching the dog tags, and saluting the boots, helmet, and rifle.

Every memorial services makes me more disgusted with this pageant. Every flashbulb that snaps a photo of a full bird in new boots, clean uniform, and shaven blue saluting for his photo op makes me ill. At one service, a Sergeant Major asked the photographer to take another because he thought his salute was off. I'm not joking. This is a "memorial"? This is how we make amends to our dead? The "VIPs" for a memorial service are not Generals and Colonels and Sergeants Major. The VIPs are the mates of the dead, his crew, his squad, his platoon, his company, his battalion. The Soldiers closest to him, that held him in his last moment, covered in his blood as they tried to save him, they are the ones who should pay respects first. The brass can wait at the back for their photo op.

How do you honor your dead? I've been thinking of that a lot. We've had great success lately. We snatched up the #3 high value target for our Brigade (he's our Battalion's #1 most wanted) and four of his close associates the other week. Hit his office the next night, snatching a few more of his friends and grabbing documents, names, and bank account information. Hell, even criminals keep books... surprisingly good ones. Two days later, we picked up two more of his top underdogs while they were trailing one of our patrols. Hint: if you're trying to "tail" someone, don't do it from five feet away, and when they make a quick u-turn to see if they are, in fact, being followed, don't whip around right behind them. We've taken down three quarters of this man's cell on our own: our own hits, our own intel, our own command and control.

And it all matters for one reason: they killed our boys, our friends, our brothers. This isn't one of those generalizations. These are the assholes who planned, funded, and executed the attacks on our guys. The big fish we caught was responsible for at least eight of the Battalion's deaths, including two from my company. How he came back alive is a miracle.

We're still hunting for one: the sniper, the one responsible for Fig and Harper. We want him, and we want him badly. Despite what the papers and the news and the Generals say, this is a nasty, brutal, hate-filled war. Every time there's a memorial service, you hear the same thing: You honor the fallen with your actions and how you carry on. Do what's right and don't give in to anger.

So we make our own amends. We bust our ass to break their backs. We track them, we hunt them, and then we come for them in the middle of the night, in their houses, where they feel safe and secure, with anger and violence. We come for them, snatch them away from their families, and snatch them from the arms of wives, mothers, children, carrying them off into the night into the unknown terror. We come for them, steel-eyed and stone-faced. We come for them, and we come for them, and we come for them. They took our brothers and we come for them. Away from pomp and circumstance we make our own amends.

# Part IV:
# The Worst Day

*I graduated from West Point on May 28, 2005. It was one of the happiest days of my life. It was the culmination of four years of hard work and sacrifice. It was the start of my career. The whole world was in front of me and I had stars in my eyes.*

*May 28, 2007 will forever be the worst day of my life, a day filled with pain, violence, and blood. It was the first time I ever saw a fellow Soldier seriously wounded right in front of me. It was the first time I killed someone. It was the first time in my life I felt utterly helpless. It was the first time I felt like a complete failure. I carried that day heavily for years. Even now, I can still close my eyes and watch the whole thing replay in fire and blood.*

*That day changed my life. It was the day the last of my innocence died. It was the day that seared the war onto my soul.*

*It was also the day I started to lose my shit.*

### Email: May 29, 2007 (Day 220)

The 28th of May was a day that changed my life forever. It was the worst thing I've ever experienced. It was a day that seared itself in my mind. The sights, the sounds, the smell... the smell...

It started the same way every other day does here. I oozed myself out of bed, wishing I was somewhere other than here. Battalion gave us another FRAGO to run us further into the ground. We had just finished hacking out the new schedule and SSG Neeks had asked me if I would go out that night to give someone a break. Yeah, sure, no problem. I could use a break from paperwork and getting some patrol time in kept me sharp and usually improved my mood from the time I get to spend bullshitting with my crew. A couple hours before we rolled, I talked with SFC Akers, the 3rd Platoon PSG over a cigarette. The usual stuff: maintenance, how our battalion leadership was clueless, etc. SFC Akers is a great NCO, but he has a way of getting under your skin a lot of times. We butted heads in the past, even when I was a PL in my old company. Still, I had come to appreciate him in the past couple weeks they had been down here (they were attached to a different unit at a different FOB) because he was a great NCO and made my life a lot easier when it came to his platoon. While we spoke, I stopped and told him so. I told him, man to man, that while we hadn't always gotten along, he was a great NCO, ran a great platoon, and I was thankful for the weight he helped to take off my shoulders. He smiled and responded as he always did to officers: as a smart ass... but that was SFC Akers. I'm so glad I told him those words that afternoon.

Go time comes and after a couple hiccups with one of the other tanks we roll. SFC Akers ran point. We stop by our patrol base, drop off dinner chow for the guys and take off rolling up the road to our patrol area. I ran a crew from SFC Akers' platoon since my normal crew had just been out. Me and Andrews and Dobbs were laughing and joking in the tank, hoping for a quiet night, jamming along to the machine gun pulse drum line of a Chevelle song playing through the intercom. We make a turn onto one of the hotter stretches of road in our AO and SFC Akers stops.

"What's up man? "

"Ah shit sir, it ain't nothin', just takin a look for a sec."

"Ok, roger man, gotcha".

We roll again, and then it all started.

"Mustang Mike, this is Desperado 5, Contact IED"

"Hey, Blue 4, you ok? Blue 4, Blue 4, this is Black 5, you ok man?"

"SFC AKERS STOP YOUR TANK! HEY, AKERS! AKERS, YOU GOOD MAN?"

And that was when I realized something was wrong, no one was responding, and the tank had begun to drift off the road….

"Oh shit, Andrews, gun front! Dobbs, punch it and pull around on their left side!"

I looked over and the image burned into my mind: SFC Akers had managed to squeeze himself out of a half open tank hatch and got stuck, hanging limp, skin, clothes and face black, head dripping with blood…

"AKERS!!!! AKERS!!!! CAN YOU HEAR ME?!?!? STOP THE TANK!!! STOP THE TANK!!!!"

No movement. He has to be dead.

"Dobbs! Ram their tank and cut them off!"

Brace....

BANG!

I've never come out of a tank so fast. I jumped out of my hatch and jumped onto the top of SFC Akers tank....

"SFC Akers!!!! Can you hear me??? Are you ok???? Open your eyes!!! Look at me man, look at me!"

And I start pulling him out. Thank God he's a little guy, or he never would have fit out of the space between the cupola and the hatch. I grab him under the armpits and pull, bits of charred clothing and flesh peeling off onto my gloves. That's the strange thing about a fire. There really isn't much blood. I check for a pulse and found one, did a quick once over on him, picked him up, and jumped back over to my tank. I half lowered, half dumped him down the hatch and Andrews starts treating him.

"God it hurts.... Help me... help me sir... it hurts....."

And I see Linden's hand poking up out of the thick black smoke billowing out of the loader's hatch. I reach down and pull him up out of the tank, falling with him onto the top of the turret. There's blood all over his leg. I pull out a tourniquet and slide it onto his leg. His eyes flutter and yell at him to look at me. I slap him on the side of his face and scream for him to look into my eyes and I get ready to tighten the tourniquet.

"Linden, look at me man, you're gonna be ok, you hear me? You're gonna be ok, but this is really gonna hurt in a second? You got me?"

"Do it, sir."

More screams. I tighten the tourniquet and carry Linden back to my tank. I lower him into the turret and do a quick count. I'm missing one. Oh shit...

Peters was still trapped in the driver's hole. He's alive. The tank is still on fire. So is Peters. SSG Baker ran over from his tank to help us get Peters. It's not going well, and the clock is ticking on Akers and Linden. I tell him to do something we only ever do in an emergency: I told Baker to leave us and get Akers and Linden to FOB Loyalty as fast as they could. Diaz, Andrews, and I were staying.

Back on Peters' tank everything is going wrong. Diaz, Andrews, and I tried to have Peters open the hatch. He couldn't get it. We tried to pry it open with the tanker bar far enough to pop it so we could swing it open. No dice. I tried to have Peters drop his vision block so he could get air. He couldn't move. He was burned too badly. Diaz was holding it cracked so Peters could breathe. I was hopeful because he was talking to us. I could also see him signaling us with a little orange penlight... oh shit...

The tank was on fire again. I screamed for Andrews to throw me the fire extinguisher. I jammed the nozzle into the crack as much as I could, yelled for Peters to hold his breath and turn his head and sprayed him and anywhere else I could reach. We abandoned the hatch and tried traversing the turret over the back to get him out. The power and hydraulics were out, so we had to use the manual cranks. No luck. The gears caught on a busted screen and there was too much smoke inside. Smoke in a tank isn't like smoke in a house fire. The NBC filters had caught on fire making the smoke incredibly poisonous. We couldn't stay in to rotate the turret, we couldn't get the hatch open… and the whole time I'm trying to talk to Peters, and all I could hear was "Help me, help me, my God, help me, it burns it burns, it hurts so bad… it hurts…."

I jumped back into my tank, lined up the rear of my turret and used my tank to push the other tank's gun tube around to the rear. YES!!! We're in! We can pull him out now! ...except we found the screen that opens to the driver's hole jammed in place by two other screens mangled in the attack . I was tired, my mouth was dry, I was heaving my guts up, my lungs seizing up from the smoke, and all I could think of was throw me a fucking bone here… By this time, my old platoon had arrived along with the rest of our 3rd Platoon and seven guys were on top taking 30 second turns inside trying to pull him out. We finally get him out of the tank and me and their PL carry him on a stretcher to a waiting Bradley. He was burned badly. His skin was charred, eyes glassy, clothes burned onto his body… I held his hand and talked to him the whole way. I couldn't hear a damn word he was saying, but I knew as long as his lips moved and his eyes opened every once in awhile he wasn't dead. This much I learned: He was married with two kids, one having just been born. He had just turned 21. We go to the Aid Station at Loyalty and after I saw Peters carried away, I collapsed.

Before reinforcements arrived we'd had no security, no help, and no way to defend us unless I ran to the other tank, made it inside, and managed to bring the weapons to bear. Had we been attacked we'd have died. By the Grace of God, we weren't attacked, but later we found out we were right next to secondary bombs that didn't function properly.

Me, Andrews, Diaz, and some others got treated for smoke inhalation. The tank crew were all burned pretty badly, but they'll all live. Everyone I've run into has said I did great things, that I saved lives. The only thing I see is it took me an hour to get a burned and wounded Soldier out his tank and to medical help. The logical side of me recognizes what people are saying. I did everything I could; I controlled the situation; I provided medical treatment... but I couldn't get him out. He was calling out to me, begging me, praying to God, and I couldn't get him out. The sight of SFC Akers hanging burnt and bloody out of his hatch, the sounds of Linden moaning in pain, the smell of blood and burnt flesh... it all comes back when I close my eyes, it all comes back when my mind becomes idle. It won't go away.

The first thing they teach medics is that you cannot save everyone, and even if you do everything right people may die. The first thing they teach you as an officer is that lives hang in the balance on your actions and decisions. I can't stop second guessing myself. What if I had thought to move the gun with my tank sooner before the smoke got bad then maybe we could have pulled him out? What if I hadn't let SFC Akers talk me out of taking point? Why didn't I see the bomb? Why that road? Why us? Why them? Between people asking me how I feel and telling me I did great things I'm about ready to just snap. The things I went through will probably never fully fade from memory. Parts of it will always slip into my dreams. I just want to go home. I never want to go through that again. I never want to pull one of ours out a vehicle like that. I never want feel of helpless like that. I never again want to hear "Help me, my God, it burns, it hurts, oh God it hurts so bad....."

They're putting me and four other guys in for Bronze Stars with Valor. I don't care. I don't think any of us do. We got our boys out alive, and that's what matters. I had a real good talk with the Platoon Sergeant for our infantry platoon the other day. For those of you who don't know, the Platoon Leader may be the leader, marriage counselor, financial advisor, surrogate parent, chaplain, and guide for his platoon, the Platoon Sergeant is all those and more for the Platoon Leader. Nothing can make a 20-something LT feel better like a sit down with his Platoon Sergeant. We sat and talked and smoked and I was telling him about the guilt that I had about how it took so long to get Peters out and how I was second guessing myself after the fact and he held up a big meaty paw and stopped me mid-sentence.

"You listen to me, LT. Don't EVER question what you did that day. You jumped off your tank in the middle of sector, with no regard for your own safety, pulled two guys out, saved their lives, then had your other tank run them to help, left yourself defenseless, worked like a madman to get our boy out, and never once stopped trying to get Peters out. You didn't leave him, you did everything you could to get him out till help came, and not once did you pause or even hesitate to consider yourself or anything else. You got 'em all out, got 'em all to help, and never once left Peters till the medics took him. Don't EVER think you didn't do enough or you didn't do the right thing. You are one HELL of an XO, and I'm proud to serve with you."

I stubbed out my cigarette and he wrapped me in a big, sweaty, platoon sergeant bear hug, and then I went to my room, sat down, and cried. They say time heals everything. I can't sleep. Every time I close my eyes I see SFC Akers hanging out of his hatch. I hear Linden groaning in pain. I see Diaz pulling on the hatch with all his strength screaming and crying as he tries to get to Peters, tries to reach his buddy. Your mind does strange things in contact. Time slows down, speeds up, makes funny jumps. Some things are fuzzy when you recall them and others are clear as day, bright and vivid, replaying like a movie of the damned. I have never experienced terror, despair, anger, and just plain outright violent rage as I did that day. I was scared shitless, waiting for my turn to die. I was shaking as I got into my tank to come back from the aid station at the end of it all.

Usually my emails have some sort of political commentary, moral question, or insight into our lives over here. Not this one. There isn't any deeper meaning or overall point to this one. We were scared out of our minds. The only thing we thought about was getting our boys out. If we had come under contact, I have no doubt that me, Andrews, and Diaz would have made the enemy pay dearly to get to that hatch and to Peters. We would have died right there with Peters on the front slope if it meant not leaving him to the enemy, because no matter what, you never, and I mean NEVER, leave another Soldier behind. The Soldier doesn't fight for his country, or any ideals, or any other lofty goal. He fights for his friends and brothers on the left and right, and at the end of the day, everybody comes home. It might be alive and whole, it might be hurt, or it might be in a flag draped coffin, but dammit, EVERYBODY comes home... everybody comes home.


## **Email: June 15, 2007 (Day 237)**

"To Trudge: the slow, weary, depressing yet determined walk of a man who has nothing left in life except the impulse to simply soldier on."
*-A Knight's Tale*

Sara sent me that quote one day over instant messenger. Perfectly describes our unit's current deployment situation. We are trudging. I am trudging. The whole Army is trudging. So, since this whole shit show has become a trudge, I am using this to email to focus on some happier moments from the last couple weeks:

-Watching my Commander rock out on Guitar Hero II on my X-Box, complete with black and mild hanging out of his mouth puffing smoke in the air as he played Sting's "Message in a Bottle".

-We're killing the enemy slowly but surely.

-Watching a mini-tornado sweep through the motor pool, steal some unlucky guy's cover, and he chased it all around for a full five minutes.

-We're getting food shipments into the mess hall again.

-Not being dead.

-Wrestling with SFC Adams's in the CP while I gave Crocodile Hunter style commentary.

-SFC Adam finally getting those big, meaty paws on me during my commentary.

-SFC Adam throwing me across the CP with said big, meaty paws ("CRIKEY, the strength of the grizzly is just simply amazing!").

-Finally feeling somewhat rested.

-Officially being over halfway done with deployment.

It may not seem much, but sometimes it's just the little things that have to keep you going. This is especially true due to the recent death in the company. Please pray for the family of SGT Caleb Christopher. He was killed last week by a roadside bomb. His death took a big toll on the company. So now, we're trudging, trying to get by day by day, and hanging on to any rumors or rumors of rumors we hear about redeployment. For people who regularly leave the wire, whether it be infantry, tankers, or the guys who run our supply convoys, extension means having to SURVIVE that much longer. That is the hardest part of the extension: physical, mental, and emotional survival.

I talked to my 1SG last night about dealing with what happened to SFC Akers. He looked at me and said: "Sir that will be with you for the rest of your life. You'll never forget it. One day, you may just be sitting around and all of a sudden, bam, it hits you all over again. What matters is not locking it all away, but dealing with it. It's how you deal with it and not allowing it to deal with you." He was right. 1SG's usually are. 1SG's and senior NCOs are funny that way. Like my old Platoon Sergeant told me: "Sir, for a lot of these kids, we take over where their parents left off." Nowhere is that more true than the senior NCOs in the company. Being a 1SG or a Platoon Sergeant is a lot like being a father, and that day Top told me the same things my father would have if he had been there. It was one of those times that I felt woefully immature and unqualified to do my job. Here I am, supposed to outrank this man, and he's telling me how this is all supposed to work. It's amazing how much this whole thing has aged me. I'm too young to feel this old.

**Email: June 30, 2007 (Day 252)**

Sorry it's been so long since I've written. We've been in commo black out for about a week now. In the past week seven more American Soldiers from my FOB have lost their lives, including two from my battalion. It's been a rough haul. Things are changing around here. Both sides are desperate: the militia is desperate because we're hunting them at a much higher pace. Our side is desperate from mounting pressure back home to show results and the increased tempo strains everything: men, equipment, and logistics. Either way, when it's all said and done, we'll leave, the militias will take over, both sides will declare themselves the "winner", give medals to all people of rank, and leave the little people left to sort through the mess of their own lives. Have we lost in Iraq? Have we won? I don't think either of those terms apply. You "win" at sports, you "win" in competition, you "win" when you take that hill. Winning is something concrete, objective.

What have I won? Experience, knowledge, development... and flashbacks, nightmares, and a rundown body. The guy on the other side, also fighting for what he believes, has won prison time (or death), friends and family killed, job lost, and life ruined. Like the saying goes, when those in power say a price is worth it, you can be damn sure they aren't going to be the people paying.

Other than my growing disgruntlement at a situation that is not fixable by throwing bullets or money at it, I'm doing okay. The word is that we'll be home sometime in December, but no word on whether it will be before or after Christmas. Our gear is being shipped back awhile before that, so I may end up spending my last month in Kuwait (fingers crossed). Either way, I want to go home. War is real exciting when you hear the stories, see the clips, and do the training runs... But when you get to it and have the first bullet whizz by your head the truth hits you: there is no pause, no rewind, no "do overs". You begin realize the only important thing is getting back home. That's the bottom line. I want to go home.

## **Journal: July 7, 2007 (Day 259)**

I should be happy now. I should only have 79 days left in this God forsaken shit hole of a country. Instead, I have 171 days left, just under six months to go. I can't help but think what this war has done to the Army. My best friends will separate for over a year just barely a year after they'd gotten married. Katie will have to leave her baby at four months old, and Jim will not only be a new father, but a de facto single parent as well. You look at what this war has cost the people who've fought it: broken bodies, broken minds, broken hearts, spirits, and souls, broken homes, broken lives... all because we raised our hand and volunteered to serve our country. This war has taught me so many things. It's shown me the true value of life: family, friends, someone to love... These are the things that are truly important. Many of the things we place value on simply aren't valuable in the least.

I went out on a patrol today. My first real patrol since the day SFC Akers was wounded. I don't count the dismounted raid from the JSS. There's a reason I became a Tanker, dammit. I'll take my dismounting in small amounts. I found the patrol strangely relaxing. For three glorious hours I wasn't "LT" or "XO." For three glorious hours I wasn't a patrol leader or even a tank commander. For three glorious hours I was just another dismount. It was great. All I had to do was follow SSG Simes when he got out of the truck, pull security, and search a couple houses. Looking back, I don't think it was the patrol that was so relaxing, but the lack of responsibility, not having anyone depend on me, and not having to have the answer.

I'm still not sleeping well. Nightmares, waking up screaming, crying myself to sleep... At least I didn't get the shakes again when I went out today. I don't know what the problem is. It isn't fear. I guess it's the accumulated jumpiness of too many close calls. I'd kill a man for a good nights sleep. Everything keeps building and building. I need a break. I need a win. I need something good to happen, and I need it soon. I want to go home.

## Email: 8/15/2007 (Day 298)

Right now we are at the "Golden Time" of the deployment... and when I say "Golden Time" I mean the time when people are sick and tired of dealing with each other, working 16 hour days without days off, and going stir crazy while simultaneously ceasing to care. Yes, we are in the last two months of deployment.... oops, I mean last five months. This is normal for the tail end of any deployment. The big problem is that we are NOT at the tail end. We are only 2/3 done (feels like I've been gone forever and a day, hasn't it?). It's getting ugly

Apathy is an interesting thing. Few on this email list have firsthand experience of the hours we're pulling. You literally work from sun up to sun down and do the same thing every day. Compounding it is the high level of violence, the dangerousness of the area, and the high casualty rate, not just of our own Battalion, but on Rustamiyah in general. People die here at Rustamiyah, frequently and badly, in ways that never leave you after you see them. Rustamiyah is drowning in blood.

Personally, it's hard to keep my own apathy at bay. Five months is a long push. It's like we're stuck in place and aren't going anywhere. In fact, this is the third time we've been at the five to six months remaining mark: First in April (just before we got extended, then in June and July (just before we found out that our redeployment date got switched and pushed back to January), and now again in August. So, from April to August (four months) we have bounced back and forth between five and six months left. You can see how that may start to wear on you. Despite the tour length, "half way" feeling doesn't really kick in until the six month mark (psychological thing I guess). So, compound that with the "six month mark" lasting four months, casualty rate, broken systems, and long work hours, and it's easy to see why our Battalion shuffles around like the dead man walking the green mile.

Only five more months till I'm home in the land of English, cold beer, and a population who isn't thinking about killing me every time I drive down the street. And if you think I'm exaggerating on that last part, let me tell you about the Internet Guy. The Internet Guy on the FOB has been here for a long time, has tons of certificates of appreciation from units that have been here, and has multiple U.S. citizenship endorsement letters from Battalion Commanders, Brigade Commanders, and Command Sergeants Major. He was arrested the other day for selling information on the FOB and troop movements to the insurgents. Like I said, I can't wait to get back where I don't have to worry about the population wanting to kill me at every turn.

## Journal: August 23, 2007 (Day 306)

It's been a while since I've written for me again. Re-reading these entries and letters I've noticed several consistent themes: anger, frustration, confusion, betrayal, hate, apathy, and exhaustion. Why is it that our worst natures come out when pressed and tested? Right now I'm experiencing something I haven't in a while: total apathy. I don't think I even can care anymore if I wanted to.

But even as I write this, I feel a strange release. Maybe it's just being tired. Maybe I really am starting to not care. Maybe it's just like Top said and I really am losing my fucking mind. It's amazing how things that would have raised all kinds of bells and whistles earlier in the deployment are now met with merely a raised eyebrow.

Oh, IED strike? No one hurt? Ok, everybody is heading back to where they came from.

You heard so and so got shot right? Yeah, he'll be fine. Going back stateside for rehab. Oh, ok.

You shot someone last night? You kill him? No? Why not? What do you mean you hit him in the ass?

It's just one dulled layer over another. Everything still feels like an uphill battle, even though we are approaching the downhill stretch. However, the downhill slide for this Battalion started months ago. Actually... it's been more of a downhill tumble than a slide. Either way, I'm glad it's almost over, or at least will be in 4 and a half more months. I miss the States. I miss home so badly.

## Email: August 8, 2007 (Day 322)

So last week we determined that, without a doubt, that I do, for a fact, scare small Iraqi children, especially little girls. I was out with Blue Platoon visiting a family in their sector when I determined this. The house we stopped at had a mother, two older girls about college age, an eleven and seven year old boy, and a seven and three year old girl. First, the eleven year old boy started crawling all over me. I thought he was just being a typical kid until I saw he was blind. It was a little strange to have this kid "seeing" me by feeling all over me and crawling up and down my body. He had this game he kept playing where he'd feel something on our body armor and try to guess what it was. It was pretty funny until he pulled the pin on the Platoon Sergeant's flash bang grenade.

So there I was, playing peek-a-boo with small Iraqi children while trying to stay calm with this kid crawling all over my gear and weapon when I noticed the three year old girl hiding behind her older sister's leg and occasionally poking her head out at me. So, I take off the sunglasses and gloves and slowly move to her, making faces and smiling while her sister tried to encourage her to shake my hand. I got about two feet away before she burst into tears and ran off crying yelling something in Arabic with the mother looking shocked and the other sister laughing. The older sister explained the little girl ran away screaming "NO! I don't want him to eat me! Don't let him eat me!" Apparently, while American school children tease each other with ghost stories of Bloody Mary and the Boogeyman, Iraqi children scare each other by saying that American Soldiers eat Iraqi children whole with that being the entire reason we're over here. Equal parts cute, disturbing, and sad.

The only other house worth mentioning that day was the last one we visited before we came back to the FOB. The house is at the edge of an old Iraqi airfield. It's one of the squatter areas of half finished mud houses. Well, the Platoon is there dropping off water, candy, food, and blueberry frosted pop-tarts and a few of us go inside. The father brings out his youngest: a baby so small you could still sit it in the palm of your hand. Cute little sucker. So he's looking at me, I'm looking at him, I take off the glasses and gloves and hold out a finger...... which he presently latches to with the strongman grip and pulls himself over to me..... Only to attempt to latch onto and gnaw on my knuckle.... and my glasses... and then my OTV.... Yeah, kid had one strong grip too. Took me a while to pry him off. And there he was, happily drooling and smiling away trying to see if what the fellow Iraqi babies say is true: that the brown people in the funny looking clothes really do taste like chocolate. Well, sorry kiddo, I may taste like stale sweat and dust, but definitely not chocolate, and after a three hour patrol in the 120 degree heat, I probably don't smell too great either.

    Every now and then you have moments like those to offset the rest of the stuff you see over here. It's especially helpful now that we've entered into, what seems to be, the eternal uphill climb to going home. You know, usually, when you're in something miserable that lasts a long time, there's a sense of downhill when you get near the end. I have four months left of a 15 month deployment, and the general feeling over here is that we must have missed the turnoff for the downhill because every day it gets tougher and tougher to keep going. One way or another, nothing lasts forever (except death and taxes) and this too shall pass.... and when it does, I'm taking a vacation... and by vacation I mean plopping on the couch, drinking an ice cold beer, eating pizza, and not doing a thing. I can almost see it now.

# Part V:
# Going, Going...

*I was at rock bottom.*

*Well, I THOUGHT I was at rock bottom. The real rock bottom hadn't come yet.*

*I was not well. I wasn't sleeping. I kept having nightmares. Flashbacks. I couldn't close my eyes without seeing a personal horror show of the worst moments of the deployment. I was pissed off at everything and everyone, most of all myself. I still blamed myself for what happened to Akers, Linden, and Peters.*

*I was losing my mind. Still, what had I gone through that everyone else around me hadn't? What was wrong with me? Everyone else is fine, so I must just be weak. Suck it up, drink water, rub some dirt on it, and walk it off, Trooper. If you need a distraction there's always more work to do.*

*I didn't want to be seen as the pussy that went to the Combat Stress docs on the FOB while everyone else kept fighting. Little did I know at the time, but NONE of us were fine. In fact, we were getting worse by the day. We were far beyond fine, as individuals, as a group, and as a unit. No one can go through the level of violence and death we had been seeing regularly and be fine. We still had a job to do. There'd be time for sorting myself out on the back end. I was sure of it. Just get home and everything would be fine. I'd be fine.*

**Journal: September 19, 2007 (Day 333)**

I think I'm losing my mind.

**Email: September 30, 2007 (Day 344)**

The last few days were nothing but hair pulling stress and I'm glad they're over. We had to close down the JSS. Now keep in mind that this compound was built up over eight months. We had a lot of crap. The Army tends towards pack rat tendencies. Our vehicles looked like gypsy wagons. Bradleys meant to hold troops were crammed full of tat boxes, cots, mattresses, and anything else we could shove into whatever space was available. At the start of it all, both Majors at Battalion looked at me and said "Here you go, plan and synch this major battalion level movement. By the way, we want you to pull everything out… including the PVC pipe that you had dug into the ground for your shower trailer." Did I mention the Battalion Commander gave me 48 hours to close up shop?

That's how Operation Saigon came to be. Yes, I was the one who named it. Somehow it stuck while drawing no more than a heavy sigh of irritation from the Battalion Commander. My Commander thought it was hilarious. Despite my best efforts, they denied my request for a Huey to fly over on the last day and pick me up from the roof. I planned to have my Stetson on, complete with cowboy boots and spurs, and hang onto the helicopter's skids from one hand while waving a giant American flag from the other… but I digress. In all reality, it was a giant pain. The biggest pain wasn't packing, it was the Iraqi Police.

Iraqi Police are like locusts. If it isn't bolted down with a guard on it, it will get stolen. Hell, even if you

HAVE a guard on it and it's under triple lock and key, they'll find a way to steal it. Upon hearing that the Iraqi Police were looting government property (as soon as they saw us packing it was "Mister, mister, you give me, you give me one. Can I take this?") the Battalion XO demanded to know how we could let this happen. Why weren't guards posted? Well sir, we do have a guard on it, but the guy goes to the bathroom and within three minutes the Iraqi Police have stolen a stack of plywood, 15 nets, a weight set, AND the porta-potty the guy was peeing in… with him in it. These guys are crafty. I've known some thieving, sticky fingered kleptomaniacs in my day, but none of them have anything on these guys.

Finally came the big night to haul everything away. When I finally managed to pick up my local national operated crane (After I tracked them down…. Then after they had dinner…. Then after they stopped to pray in the middle of the road…. Then after they got the crane started… oh yeah, all that happened while we were on FOB Loyalty) things went pretty smoothly. Meanwhile, I spent my time running to and fro trying to keep the largest logistical mission I've done from collapsing on its own weight. I don't even want to get into many more details except to mention that the JSS gave me a final parting gift: stepping into the shower sewage runoff as I stumbled to my truck in the dark to leave. Nothing like an hour ride back with the smell of raw sewage on your foot. Mmmmmm.

I'm sitting at 93 days left until I fly out of Iraq. When I'll actually be home, I don't know. Rest assured, if I can be woken from my bed I will have my cell turned on the next day. Almost home.

## Email: October 22, 2007 (Day 366)

On October 22, 2006, I stepped on a plane and left everything I know and love and left for the far side of the world. On October 22, 2007, I should step off a plane and return to everything I know and love. On October 22, 2007, I am sitting in the same chair, in the same room, in the same country that I will continue to sit in for another 2 months. I should be done. I am not.

It's a very hard thing to take an honest look back at a year of your own life. It's even harder still to take that look and barely recognize yourself. I stepped on that plane ready to save the world and bring Democracy, Coca-Cola, and Wrangler Jeans to Iraq. I sit older (much older than a year would lead you to believe), wiser (much wiser than a year should have made me), and infinitely more tired (much more tired that any year could have left me).

I've gone through too many phases to count since I've been here: Excitement, trepidation, anger, bitterness, resolution, hate, rage, acceptance, resignation, hope, and apathy. I've seen and done things I'd never thought I'd do, and hope I'll never have to do again. I plumbed the depth of what I thought myself "incapable of," stood on both sides of the moral coin, and tried to make right out of a losing situation. I've given money to a poor family and put a gun in an old man's face, all in the same day, and all in the same patrol. I've had dinner with an Iraqi family and tossed the kitchen of another. I've acted on the intent to kill that lives in my heart and ordered my Soldiers to gun down people fighting for the wrong flag. I've chased men through the streets, dragged women and children out of their homes, and hunted under the street lights of Baghdad. I've given food, I've given medicine, and I've given aid. I've felt myself become sick and felt myself laugh over the same actions. I've looked upon people with an unquenchable hate and an unfathomable pity. I have felt my soul torn over decisions made and not made, things I've done and things I didn't, and all the time I realized that the only truth in war is that war IS hell.

I've wiped my own tears. I've wiped the tears of my Soldiers. I've washed blood from my hands and gloves, sometimes mine, sometimes the enemy's, and sometimes my Soldiers'. I've pulled a man out of a burning tank. I've sat in my room and screamed in terror and frustration as JAM shelled our FOB. I've lost control. I've regained it. I have memories I will treasure and others I pray to God to take away.

Through it all, one thing has become a clear reality. There is no "glory" in war. Concepts of glory, valor, and honor are the things we sell to ourselves to put one foot in front of the other during these times. If you ask any person decorated for valor, they'll probably tell you the same thing: I'd rather have not gotten the medal and still have my friends with me. The only glorious thing in war is the bonds that develop between people trudging alongside each other. We cross the finish line together or not at all. No one is left behind. And it isn't pretty. And it isn't nice. And it isn't patriotic. Politicians and Generals can pound the pulpit about moral obligation and political justifications all they want. Ask the Soldier what the goal of deployment is and you'll get one answer: To get home again.

All a Soldier ever longs for is to get home. Everything is window dressing. Love for home and love for his comrades keeps you going when you're cold, when you're tired, when you're hungry. Every task, every mission, every order is not completed for its sake alone. It's done because it gets you one step closer to home.

Is this the definitive answer? No. Am I right? Maybe. Does it matter? Not at all. This is just one soldier's opinion. This is my view after a year of fighting the enemy outside the wire, the enemies inside my Battalion, and the enemies within my heart and soul... and now it's time to finish the job.

### Email: November 14, 2007 (Day 389)

I don't know if I ever mentioned this or not, but we have a dog living with the company now. It first came around about a month ago, and after being fed a healthy diet of beef jerky and canned chicken it decided it liked us enough to hang around. Now, the dog is an official member of the company. It has not one, but TWO collars (a flea one and a regular one), gets regular baths (I'm not kidding), and sleeps in peoples rooms. It seems to have an affinity for the big plush chair I inherited, as at least once a day I will hear it scratching at the door, demanding entrance, only to trot into my room, hop up onto my chair, sprawl out, and give a look of shocked indignation when I scoot it over so I can sit down. It then sprawls half on top of me while I rub its belly and feed it jerky until it passes out, and once it wakes up, demands I play with it. It's almost like having a small piece of home here with us.

I'm a little over a month and a half away from RIP/TOA, and about two months before I will be back Stateside and I had the realization that, very soon, I will have to adjust to life in the World. After almost 15 months, THIS life has become normal. I do the same thing, day in day out (you could almost set a watch by the schedule I keep), my money magically stacks up in banks accounts, I pay my one bill with one click online every month, and my life is generally run for me.

Sara returning has made me realize that I will have to adjust back to the real world. You think it'd be easy to go from a situation where you're working 24/7 with a constant fear of death to being back in civilization with normal working hours and weekends. I am sort of terrified of going home. Will I adjust ok? Will I leave all this behind me over here? Will I be one of those guys tweaking out during war movies or diving under my bed when a car backfires? Will I start sleeping again? Will the nightmares stop? Will everything still fit when I get back? What if it doesn't? What's changed, what hasn't? Have I changed?

It hit me when Sara told me that she found it irritating that she finally had a nice, comfortable bed but couldn't fall asleep because she was used to sleeping on a hard, beat up mattress for over a year. I look at house pictures, Ikea web pages, Best Buy ads, and every inch of me is straining at the leash to get home... and every inch is just as worried what that will be like. Will it be like mid tour leave when I froze in my tracks at Disney World because I saw an Arab man who looked exactly like a body I pulled out of an abandoned storage area? Will I just fall back into step with no problems? I guess it's all just rational/irrational fear. Symptoms of an overly active mind trying to guess, strategize, and anticipate every facet of its life, despite knowing it's an impossible and useless task.

Days are growing shorter and colder. Paranoia is growing in the air. Like they always say, if you're going to buy it, it's always on the last patrol right before you go home. Let me tell you, survival instinct is kicking in big time around here. It doesn't make it any easier that I'll be eating my second Thanksgiving in a row in a chow hall halfway around the world. It doesn't make it any easier that I'm looking at the second Christmas tree I've set up here. It doesn't help that when I spoke to one of my civilians friends on the phone they asked where I was, and when I said Iraq, their response was "Are you serious? You've been there like, forever. I thought you were supposed to be home already?" Yeah, me and about 800 other guys thought we'd be home by now too. I'm not angry, I'm not bitter... I'm just tired. Very, very tired. I want to go home. There's no place like home.

### Email: November 16, 2007 (Day 391)

On November 11th my class lost another classmate. He died of wounds suffered during an ambush. He was 24.

The oddest thing about the military is that you live your lives at what seems like an accelerated rate. You start your career early, people marry early, have children early, grow old early, and, God forbid, die early. I look around at all my classmates who are already married, and then the ones who already have kids or are expecting. I look at 28 year old Staff Sergeants who look like they're damn near 40 and who's bodies feel like they're 60. I look at the lists in Stars and Stripes: KIA at 19, KIA at 21, KIA at 26, KIA at 22. A lot of times, it just seems surreal. We all knew what we were doing when we raised our hand and took our oath, but like a friend said to me today: "We're too young to die."

We're too young to die. That's what it boils down to. My friend's sister (she was Class of 2003) was killed in action at the age of 24 while we were in OBC. My friend and classmate, Thomas Martin, who would be home by now and married in the spring, is dead at 27. Killed in action. Died of wounds. Non-combat related death. All terms heard on a daily basis and all terms that fail in capturing the event's significance. It always fails to convey the impact of the event.

It's hard to think about your own mortality, even harder to accept, and even harder coming to peace with. At times I was sure I would die. Other time I didn't care if it happened or not. I've nearly broken my own neck running from incoming mortars. I've ridden with half my body out of the hatch through a sniper hot spot while smoking a cigarette, regarding the bullet that struck just short with nothing more than a passing interest. All in all, I don't know what to tell you. I can't really explain it. All I can say is caring about life or death eventually becomes, simultaneously, the most important and most tiring thing occupying your world. I can't really figure out how to put it into words. This is all very confusing.

Part of you knows this is coming, that it could happen, and that you knew what you got into. The other half is steadily shouting back that it's all unfair. I think both sides are right... but no one ever said life was fair. Like my friend said, we're too young to die. She's right; we are too young to be dying. Unfortunately, neither life nor the war care about fairness.

### Journal: November 17, 2007 (Day 392)

We're getting older. We're marrying, we're conceiving, we're dying. Seven of my classmates lay in the ground, not even three years from commissioning. Numerous classmates are married. More are engaged. A few are expecting. Some even have children. I have a goddaughter. The numbers grow when I look at the ones I went to high school with. Married. Children. Engaged. Careers. Moving. Onward. Upward. Outward. We're scattering to the winds. We're going off into the world. I sit here and wonder when it all changed. When high school ended, we swore that college wouldn't change anything. That'd we'd be together forever, no matter what. It was the same thing at the end of college, just with a different set of friends.

Where did the time go? One second, I'm sitting out on the deck of the coffee house, skateboards and punk rock in the parking lot, hooded sweatshirts, torn jeans, and skull caps, haze of cigarette smoke in the air. I blinked and I'm sitting in the Firstie Club, catching my Armor insignia at the end of a chugged beer, talking about how we couldn't wait to be Platoon Leaders in combat. When I went to sleep, I woke up when someone shook me on a cot at NTC telling me the Commander needs me in the CP for a mission. I drift off for a second, and when I open my eyes I'm on a couch, the woman I love sleeping with her head in my lap while I stroke her hair. I let my eyes close to join her and I wake up in a church as the best man on the day of my best friend's wedding, telling him he'll do just fine as a husband and, one day, as a father. I go to bed after the wedding and wake up to the sound of explosions, my Platoon Sergeant pulling me half naked out of bed to get me to the bunker before the next barrage hits. I shut my eyes to block out the noise, and open them to a picture of a tiny human life being held by her parents and the card introducing me to my goddaughter.

When I was in high school my dad would always tell me to slow down and not be in such a rush to grow up, that these were the best years of my life, and once they passed, they'd never come back. He was right. I grasp at memories, clutching them tight, hoping they'll never fade. I'm torn between building a life with the woman I love and my new family, and the life that I grew away from. For the first time that life I keep wishing things would slow down and let me catch my breath.

I never thought growing up would be like this. I thought it would be a gradually progression of things moving from deep sentiments to fond memories, a steady realization of age and responsibility, and a confident acceptance of life ahead. Instead, it felt like a jarring kick. The first time I realized it, was when me and my old Platoon were sitting in the middle of an enemy compound surrounded, and they looked at me and said "Sir, what do we do?" Since then, it's only gotten worse.

What happened to wonder and innocence? When did I become jaded? When was the last time I looked in mirror and saw light instead of hate and burnout? When did I stop being a child? When did I stop being a young man? When did I become an adult?

I sit here in my room, neglected cigarette turned to ash, and I wonder. I wonder, and I wish, and I realize that my father was right all along. Those were the best years of my life, and I can't get them back. I have to let them become fond memories, instead of a distant longing, or I'll never move forward. Still, I wouldn't mind having one day back there again, for old time sake.

## Journal: November 18, 2007 (Day 393)

Today I thought I was going to die. In fact, I was sure of it. This morning's paper carried the headline of "Baghdad to be turned over to Iraq in beginning of '08. Security greatly increased." This morning we took 16 rockets, the majority slamming into two of the Battalion TOCs on the FOB, including ours. This morning, in the span of 40 minutes, five FOBs and COPs were struck by indirect or direct fire and an IED hit a patrol out on RTE Plutos. This morning showed that the enemy could still hit with coordination to devastating effect. I guess the guys who did it never got the memo about Baghdad's improving security situation.

I'm so close to home now it's driving me crazy. The desire to go back has turned into a gnawing hunger. I want normalcy. This isn't normal. This isn't life. This can't be real. This isn't happening. This is all just a bad dream. I keep wishing I could close my eyes and wake up back in my bed, Sara's head on my chest, her hair tickling my nose, her body's warmth against my skin. I want this to have all been a dream. I want all the scars to have been nightmares. I want my fucking life back. I feel robbed. I feel cheated.

I laid on the floor this morning, body armor on, listening to the shrill screams of incoming rockets, the buzz of an Apache's cannon, the cracks of rifle fire. I was sure this was it. I said my goodbyes, said my prayers, and prayed I would die like a man. I knew it was coming. I'd been too lucky, and I was about to go home. You always die right before you go home. Life is cruel that way. I just want to go home.

### **Email: November 21, 2007 (Day 396)**

I have 41 days of deployment left to go, and before I get home, I will die.

I have 41 days of deployment left to go, and when I get home, I will be alone.

I have 41 days of deployment left to go, and somewhere in there, I will fail in my mission to redeploy us.

There. I've said them. Now with that out the way I can get on with what I have to do. A smart, gruff, retired Sergeant First Class told me before I left that the only people who say they aren't afraid are liars and fools. He was right. I've been terrified more times than I can count since I've been over here. What did I do a few days ago, during a massive mortar attack? Did I drop to the floor and throw my gear on and get under cover? No, I stayed in my bed, rolled towards the wall, and pulled the blankets over my head, just like you do when you're a little kid, believing not seeing it makes it all go away. I laid under my blankets and shook as I saw the flashes from the impact under the crack in my door. I laid there and gave my final confession to God, knowing that the next one would hit my room, and I would die.

Fear is a powerful thing. It can galvanize you to action, or freeze you in place. When everything is stripped away, it boils down to the most ingrained instinct in all life on the planet: fight or flight. We can say what we want for training, tactics, and experience. Survival instinct is one of the most powerful driving forces people have. Everything Soldiers are conditioned and trained to do can only override that for so long. You see it every day in my Battalion. Leaders take fewer risks, real patrols occur less and less often, people are less likely to move to the sound of the guns and press the attack. You hear it everywhere: "I've only got 41 days left. What's the point anymore?"

Yesterday, the Battalion took another hit. A platoon out in sector was hit by a roadside bomb, killing one Soldier and one interpreter. Three more were seriously injured, with one losing the lower half of his jaw and part of his arm, another having both legs broken, and another that took so much shrapnel that they don't think any amount of surgery will remove it all. This happened with 42 days left in a deployment that should have been over last month... and that's the word whispered through the halls, passed between glances in the chow hall: If we hadn't been extended, our brother would still be alive, and these guys would be going home in one piece. That's the cruelest hurt of all, because it's true on two sides of the coin. It's true that this could have happened at any time, and it's no one's fault it happened now. It is also true that if we had been home, they'd be drinking beer with us instead of laying in an ER or in a flag draped coffin. And lurking in the shadows of it all is the fear. If it could happen to them, on just any typical day, it could happen to me. I could die right before I leave. I could never see home, wife, family, and friends ever again.

The three fears I listed at the start are fears I struggle with every day. I'm afraid to die now that I've found something to live for. I'm afraid when I go home I won't be able to reconnect because I've been away too long, changed too much, and I'll be all alone. I'm afraid I'll fail for some unforeseen reason and the unit's redeployment will get screwed up. Fear only has power as long as you let it. As long as it stays buried, it can continue to feed and grow and wait in the recesses of your mind. Admitting your fear is the first step to facing it, to overcoming it, to master it. Life is a matter of choices. Every day, life gives us new choices to make. We are not victims of circumstance; we are victims of our own choices. I choose to face my fear.

### Email: December 19, 2007 (Day 424)

You hear it all the time in speeches about the war:

"We're wasting our soldiers' lives in an Iraqi Civil War."

"If we pull out now, then the sacrifices and deaths of our military men and women will have been for nothing."

It's shouted in every corner, pushed from every pulpit, and bullied by every pundit. Each side, each facet, and each political stripe: If we don't leave/stay then our soldiers' deaths will have meant nothing. Even in death, the soldier is shifted like a pawn by his Statesmen. Each wound, each death, each tragedy is another bit of ammunition for the next election. The President praises those who make the ultimate sacrifice and Congress blasts him for continuing to demand those sacrifices.

Soldiers do not fight for political motives. Soldiers do not carry out orders for the sake of foreign policy. They certainly do not break their bodies for the sake of their elected leadership. Soldiers fight for each other. They fight for the man on their left and right. The guy they carry out of the burning vehicle is the same man they carried home from the bar before they left on deployment. The man he cries with is the same man he cried with when his wife left. The man he misses is the friend he came through the ranks with. As long as soldiers give of themselves so the man on their left and right can live, no Soldier's death will ever be for nothing.

This war has become ugly. It's ugly back home and even uglier on the ground. However, we must never forget that behind each casualty report, each statistic, and each fire fight is a family, wife, mother, father, son, daughter, sister, and brother who's life has crashed down while we casually flip the channel on the TV. We will never falter, and we will never quit, but, many times, the rest of our country seems content to forget.

# Part VI:
# ...Gone

*This is it. I was finally on my way out of Iraq! Just a couple of more weeks and I'd be home in my own bed holding my girlfriend. I was home. It was over. The war is behind me.*

*I should have sought help right away, but I didn't.*

*Every soldier takes a Post Deployment Health Assessment (PDHA) upon returning from down range. The PDHA includes sections pertaining to mental health issues and a soldier can use it to say they needed help. Regrettably this didn't always happen. High volume and too few qualified mental health professionals was a perfect combination for long wait times, zero continuity in soldier care, and soldiers unable to get help when it mattered the most. Instead of therapy, the Army fell back on an "easy" solution: medication. It took longer to get cognitive behavioral therapy than it did to get a two month supply of Xanax and Ambien. Hey, your back hurts from deployment too? Here's 30 days of Vicodin before you head on home.*

*This is not to say that chaplains, healthcare professionals, and other support staff were uncaring. I know countless chaplains, doctors, nurses, and individual Army leaders who made herculean efforts to help the soldiers they could. Unfortunately, the system was broken at the institutional level. The Army was simply unprepared by the sheer volume of soldiers needing help and did not have adequate resources to help them. And this is just the soldiers.*

*Imagine being a family member or spouse trying to seek counseling because you have to watch someone you love slowly lose their mind in front of you. Imagine fearing your spouse, someone who never raised their voice before, who now has unpredictable mood swings that can turn violent at any second. Who do you turn to for support?*

*Hey, the soldiers are the ones with the real problems, not you, right? Right? All around us soldiers, spouses, significant others, and families shuffled along under the growing weight of our collective, willful ignorance. Things were not ok. People needed help. We needed to support each other.*

*None of that entered my mind at the time. The war would be behind me. The blood, death, violence... none of that will matter anymore. It all got left in Iraq and I won't have to deal with it ever again. My life can go back to normal.*

*Was that a realistic expectation? No, not by a long shot... but I didn't know any better. It was an expectation born out of horror, hope, and a deep, deep craving for salvation from my own personal hell playing out in my mind on a daily basis. It wasn't realistic in the least. Most of all, it was unfair. It wasn't unfair to me, but to the people I was coming back to. I was going to have to work on things, but I didn't see it that way at the time. All that mattered was I was home.*

*I was home. It was over. The war is behind me.*

*I was a fool...*

*... And it nearly cost me everything.*

### Email: December 24, 2007 (Day 429)

It's been a long 15 months. It's been a slog, a trudge, an exertion of the body, mind, and spirit. It's been 15 months driven by the force of will, the Grace of God, and the all consuming desire to return home again. These 15 months were the defining experience of my young life. It's been a cornerstone, another piece of the foundation of who I'll become. It's been an experience I only want to forget, but will stay with me the rest of my life. You learn a lot about yourself while you're out here. I've learned that I can lead men under fire. I've learned what it's like to feel as if you're going to die. I've learned what real fear is. Real hate. I've learned what it's like to lose control. I've learned what it's like to give into the blackness in your heart. I've learned what it's like to come back from it. I've learned deep longing for another. I've learned what it feels like to lose faith in a cause. I've learned what it feels like to gain it back again. I've learned who I am and what I want to become. I've found that I'm stronger than I thought. I've found that this comes naturally. I've found what I thought were my limits and pushed past them. I've learned to deal with loss. I've learned to control my hate, my anger, my rage. I've learned to dole out violence with the cold, distant manner of turning it into "work." I've learned to deal, learned to cope, learned to accept.

I sit here with four days left in Baghdad. I'm tired, burnt out, sick as all hell, and I'm keeping upright on a ghoulish combination of medication, caffeine, and cigarettes. I look back at what's happened over the year and I still don't know how to feel about it all. I haven't figured out how to reconcile the balance. I lied to myself when I left. I said that when I put on my body armor to roll out the wire I would put myself in a box so none of the ugliness would touch me. It isn't possible. You can't separate yourself like that. One bleeds over into the other.

What I did outside the wire would come back into my dreams at night. I was the one who shot the 14 year old boy with the detonator, not some other version of me. You can't keep it separate.

Still, there were good times. A night spent sitting on top of the OP huddled around a kerosene heater and eating chicken cooked by the woman in the apartment below. Giggling as someone trips and falls into sewage water during a raid. Playing football with the end zones and sidelines marked by tanks. Watching a driver freak out because you put the tank's gun tube into his car window when he refused to move. Laughing as a wild dog chases your wingman's tank and then gets flung across the road when it tries to bite the moving track. Poker nights with the support guys filled with under the table deals to keep the Company going.

Where do I go from here? Home I guess. Back to friends and family. Back to the World. Back to normalcy. I still have work to do in putting myself back together, not in the sense of being broken, but in the sense of reconciling the balance and finding where I stand. I want this to be over. I want to forget. I know that's impossible, but I'm human, and I can't help it. I'm ready to come home, and put this aside, if only for a year before I have to do it again. But that stretch of the rabbit hole is for me to go down and figure out.

### Email: January 06, 2008 (Day 442)

One thing I've learned about war is that it's never over. You'll always carry part of it with you. Some things will never truly go away, random snippets of instinct and habit that surface through the murk and run themselves again and again. You never quite get rid of it. For a while it may be an extreme reaction. Later along the line, it may simply be the twitch of an eye. Either way, the ghosts endure, and no amount of time or exorcism can ever fully send them away.

For a lot of the deployment, from time to time, I've had trouble sleeping. For certain periods I was a full blown insomniac. Imagine the worst moments of your life. Now imagine, that every time you close your eyes at night you see them, you hear them, you live them. Imagine that every time you hear certain words, see certain sights, or hear certain sounds, you receive a highlight reel of your own private hell. Imagine that it never goes away.

Two nights before I left Iraq, I found myself banging on a wall locker in my room. All three of my roommates were yelling for me to calm down, asking what was wrong. I had no idea what I was talking about. Apparently, I had leapt out of bed, torn the sheets and blankets off, began trashing my side of the room, and was screaming my lungs out the whole time. I didn't remember any of it. The only thing I remember was the same thing I always remember: the face of a burnt up 21 year old kid missing half his arm. I told them all I was just sleep walking and we laughed it off nervously. They went back to bed, and I stayed up outside for another two hours and chain smoked nearly a pack of cigarettes. Fast forward to last night. Wake up at 0200, mattress and sleeping bag soaked through with sweat, eyes darting around the darkened bay, reaching for a weapon that isn't there, rubbing my hands against my towel to try and get off the blood and flesh that has long since washed away.

Rewind: May 29th. Laying awake for hours, chest heaving, can't sleep, keep seeing it replay all over again like a bad movie.

Rewind: May 28th, 2007. "Mustang Mike, Desperado 5, contact IED.... tank's still rolling, doesn't look bad, will call back with SITREP." Fast forward: crouched on top of the tank with only my 9mm, aiming at the 14 years old looking kid trying to work a clacker. Breath, sight picture, squeeze, recoil, kid drops, legs jerk out of view in a cloud of dust. Did I hit him? I tell myself no. I hope no.

Rewind: December. Roll up to the same abandoned storage unit we've passed through a million times before. Roll up on a triple homicide. Pick up his head, hold it up to the light, snap the picture, wipe hands off on his shirt, try to close his eyes, they won't stay closed. Fast forward: STOP YOUR FUCKING CAR!!!! STOP YOUR FUCKING CAR AND GET THE FUCK OUT!!! One shot into the air. HANDS! HANDS! HEY MOTHERFUCKER, STOP AND GET OUT OF YOUR FUCKING- HE'S RUNNING! OPEN FIRE!!! CLEAR THE CAR!!! Over the car, though the animal stalls, round the corner, we see him behind us, sprint past the garage door, he's at the end of the row, weapon up, take aim, squeeze off a shot, see it ricochet as he gets away, kicking in a storage unit door because I'm pissed, go back and finish reducing three lives to a debrief involving a sectarian motivated triple execution.

Rewind: January. Hey whoa, hold up ya'll, I think we got something. Yep that's an IED- Mustang Mike, Cobra White One, contact IED, pushing forward, locking down the area. Hey, White 3, you ok? White 3? Out of the truck. DARREN!!! DARREN!!! Yeah, sir, I'm fine, just a little bell rung is... hey sir, where are you going? Kick in one door, then another, drag out families, old men, women, children, see the triggerman take off, chase, break into a courtyard, grab the man at the front door, where is he, he won't say, he's lying, I saw the guy run in here, drag

117

him away by his shirt collar, he tries to fight, give him a reason not too, question everyone, go home.

Now: I see it all from time to time again. I saw the executed man in a crowd at Disney world. I saw Neale in the Rustamiyah chow hall. I saw Tom standing in line at the PX down here. None of it goes away, not the things you see, the friends you lose, and the stuff you go through. It all remains in some form or another. The only thing that's still up in the air is how I will get over it all.

## **Journal: February 18, 2008 (Home for 28 Days)**

No matter how logical we try to be, we are ultimately still human, creatures of feeling and emotion. I kept telling myself that just because I come back home that all my problems would not go away, that I would have work to do, that I would not automatically be made whole. No matter how many times I said it, no matter how much I knew it to be true, no matter how many times I drilled it in my head, I still expected it. I was home. Everything should be fine… but it's not.

I'm stressed. I'm tired. I'm angry. God, I'm angry. The worst part is I don't know why. I shouldn't be stressed. I'm on leave. I shouldn't be tired. I sleep nine hours a night. I shouldn't be angry. My life is objectively superb right now. I'm used to logically diagnosing and fixing problems. Identify, evaluate, act, but it's not working. I can't do it. I don't know why I'm acting this way, and that's what makes me angrier than anything.

I still don't have a steady sleep cycle, I'm still not winding down, and, worst of all, I'm taking it out on the person closest to me. I don't understand what's wrong with me. I can't explain my actions. I can't sort my feelings. I keep trying to force a reboot, to put things back to how they were, how they should be, and I just can't do it. I'm tired of fighting, sick of worrying, and scared that I'll be stuck this way.

Have you ever looked in the mirror and not recognized the person staring back? Have you ever wondered what happened to yourself? Have you ever thought you've lost your mind? I want my life back. I want myself back. I want to be normal. People keep telling me that this is "normal" and that I'm "simply going through the typical post-deployment adjustment period" where I "readjust to my surroundings and relearn how to behave in normal society." Well, that's all well and good. Now take your empty sayings and go fuck yourself. I want my life back NOW.

I always wondered about so many things. Why guys come back and can't stop drinking. Why people hug and kiss and cry on the parade field right off the plane and get divorced a few months down the line. Why people fight so hard to get back safe only to have their lives fall apart once they return to the World. Now I know. When I was deployed, all I wanted to do was get back home to the real world, to comfort and safety, and to my family and the girl I love. Now that I'm home, I can't stop thinking that life was easier back in Iraq. Was it? Hell no. I worked like a dog every day, lived with the ever present possibility of a violent death, and had to deal with people who either wanted me dead or wouldn't lift a finger to intervene on my behalf. It wasn't emotionally easier either. I had a lot of sleepless nights, even more nightmares, and a couple times where I seriously thought about biting the barrel of my pistol.

I guess the difference is that after awhile, even though those emotions are tough and hard to deal with, at least they are a known quantity. When you return your thrust into the unknown: communication must be relearned, intimacy must be re-mastered, and a whole different set of rules and skills relating to decorum, interaction, and behavior must be brought online and restored to full functionality... and all in the midst of "Hey! I bet you're glad to be home!" and "So what was the war like?" mixed with "Well, you know what you need to do is..." and capped off with "So did you kill anybody?", and the majority of it from people who have no idea what it was like to go through what you did... and even when it comes from people who have a basis to relate, well, shit, what the hell do THEY know, because they didn't go through the same shit you did, so fuck them... and you retreat, and you clam up, and you hide in whatever manner you can. You withdraw, hoping that it will all go away and one day you'll just wake up normal and happy... Because that's what everyone wants in the end right? Happiness? And then it hits you, somewhere down the line, after you pushed everyone away, after you find yourself isolated, and after you're alone, that maybe this wasn't the right way to go.

I just want to be happy. I want my life back. I don't want to be angry. I don't want to feel socially awkward. I don't want to feel trapped. I don't want to feel like I'm constantly seething just below the surface. I just want to be normal. Is that so much to ask?

## Journal: March 18, 2008 (Home for 57 Days)

The ice clinks in the glass, another dose of liquor. I'm sick of all the pills the Army keeps giving me. Self-medication is the order of the day. Pick your poison: Jim, Jack, Jose; Camel, Newport, Marlboro; Vicodin, Percocet, OxyContin; Ambien, Seroquel, Trazadone; Xanax,

Effexor, Zoloft. You got to get up to get down. Better living through chemistry. Everything swirls in a haze. You're functional. You're "normal." You're "healthy." At least that's what they keep telling you, and themselves, so they can check you off a roster and send you packing with more meds.

What *is* normal anyways? The simple connotation of the word "normal" implies an outlier. "Normal" can't exist without "abnormal." It's defined in part by its opposite. So what makes me normal? Is it sleeping eight hours a night, having a couple drinks on weekends, and kissing my girlfriend with "Honey, I'm home" when I come in from work? So what does it mean when I'm up at oh-dark-thirty chain smoking, drinking, and writing this shitty excuse for a memoir? I thought war stories were supposed to have a happy ending? The hero comes home at the end to his waiting young wife and they live happily ever after? Or what about the patriotic version? A young man goes off to die while the young wife stands resolute in the doorway of their little home, proud of her Soldier making the sacrifice. Remember kids, Uncle Sam wants YOU!

It's not supposed to go on after the war is over. The curtain is supposed to close on the happy ending, on the reunion at the parade field, of gathering your loved one in your arms, twirling her around and kissing her. There's not supposed to be anymore after that. There's not supposed to be anger management class, divorce court, the drinking, and the pills. It's all supposed to end with the kiss on the parade field… but it doesn't. The story doesn't end on the parade field, and what was written in blood is now written in tears of frustration carried away in the unending haze from a lit cigarette as it burns down to ashes and dust.

*I came home from my first deployment on January 22, 2008.*

*I had severe problems. I was angry, drank too much, and lashed out at everyone around me, especially Sara. I had a litany of health issues stemming from the deployment. The Army drowned me in pills. At one point I was on six or seven different medications to include narcotic painkillers, anti-depressants, anti-anxiety, sleeping pills, and more. My medicine cabinet looked like a pharmacy, and most days I couldn't function without half that pharmacy pumping through my system.*

*I popped them like candy. Even better, I mixed them with my alcohol. Nervous and edgy? Xanax is miraculous. Emotions all out of whack? Zoloft and Effexor will make you incapable of giving a shit. Can't sleep? Half and Ambien and half a Trazodone will do wonders, especially when you chase it with a glass of tequila. Better living through chemistry. You gotta get up to get down.*

*I was having difficulties at work and home and they continued to mount every day. The majority of the leadership from the deployment had moved on to other places, and the new leadership at the Battalion and Brigade level possessed little patience for what they viewed as "weak" soldiers "faking" mental health issues to get out of work. Instead of ensuring soldiers got the help they needed, the new chain of command cleaned house. Guys were booted out the Army, shipped away to other unit, or, if they were lucky, told to straighten themselves out or find a new line of work.*

*Problems crept up everywhere. Soldiers who were rock steady and reliable during combat began to crack and break. Domestic violence, alcohol abuse, prescription drug abuse, depression, and suicidal ideations ran rampant in the unit, but with the climate of the Battalion guys were afraid to get help. The new Battalion Commander and Command Sergeant Major would judge you "weak" and send you packing. You were "on their team" or you were a problem, and if you had issues from the deployment you were automatically a problem.*

*I did everything the Army had told me to do. I raised my hand and said I needed help. I trusted the Army to take care of me. I trusted the Army when they said they wouldn't judge me and seeking help wouldn't hurt my career.*

*I was wrong. I was very wrong. I was wrong in such a massive way it would be comical if it wasn't tragic.*

*I sought counseling and got told the only option was group counseling. When I said I was uncomfortable with that, the mental health staff told me it was a two month wait for an individual session. After asking for a referral and making a lot of complaints I was slotted for counseling via VTC with doctors at Walter Reed. Over four sessions in a month I had three counselors. Not once did I get past the basic intake questions to talk about what was bothering me.*

*I eventually tried group therapy, hoping something, ANYTHING could help me. Plus, I figured if young soldiers saw a Captain getting help they might be encouraged to do the same. Group therapy was a sham. We came into a room, filled out questionnaires, and were called out one by one by a "counselor." He asked if I was suicidal, homicidal, and if my meds were working ok. After giving scripted one-word responses he proclaimed I was "doing fine" and they would see me in two weeks. Not once did I actually talk about what was going on with me. The whole thing took less than five minutes.*

*And I was far from fine.*

*I was living with Sara and things deteriorated by the day. The logical part of me knew I was destroying my relationship, but I couldn't seem to stop or change. For every good day there were three that were just bearable, and a couple that were downright nightmares. We fought constantly. I was sinking deeper and deeper into depression. My alcohol and pill consumption steadily increased to alarming levels. My behavior became more and more reckless.*

*My work performance and relationships took a nosedive. I was prone to angry outbursts. I was paranoid. I kept telling my bosses how bad it was getting and that I needed help. I got the same responses every time: "Suck it up", "Not this again", and my personal favorite "Just hold out until the next field problem/inspection/crisis de jour is fixed". I will never forget the day I walked into the Battalion Commander's office and told him I thought I may do something horrible if I didn't get help. He sighed and rolled his eyes. He told me to focus on my work and it'd sort itself right. You heard me right. I told my Commander I believed I may hurt myself and he responded by rolling his eyes. I was branded a problem child. Fortunately for me, I was too good at my job to chuck away. Despite being a "distraction" I was still one of the top performing officers on the staff. They couldn't afford to get rid of me.*

*That fall we went to JRTC. I came off the rails. I was losing my mind. I was fighting with my peers. Sara wasn't retuning my calls. I imploded completely. I stood up in the middle of a meeting, told everyone to fuck themselves (including the Battalion Executive Officer), walked out, and refused to do anymore work. I couldn't take it anymore. I needed out. The Chaplain, shocked at how bad I'd gotten told the Commander to send me home* on the next thing smoking before I hurt myself or someone else. That whole bus ride home the only thing I could think of was Sara. She would make it better. Get to Sara and it will all be alright. All I need to do is see her and I'll be ok.

I walked in the door and Sara left me. I barely had time to drop my bags. I cried. I screamed. I begged. I actually got on my knees and begged. Nothing. She was done. It was over.

I felt like my last support system, the person I loved the most, just threw me away. I didn't want to live anymore. I was too broken to save. I wasn't worth anything. I had no value. Everyone would be better off without me fucking up their lives and causing stress. My unit didn't want me, my chain of command didn't want me, Sara didn't want me… I didn't even want me.

There was no use being around anymore. I locked myself in the bathroom, got drunk as hell, and, tried to kill myself. I had been home for around 250 days. Sara saved my life, dragging me out of the tub and calling the ambulance. My last memory was her face and telling her I loved her.

I woke up in the hospital pissed off as all hell. Mostly, I was pissed off because I WASN'T dead. Second, the trio of men who had made my life hell and had contributed to my current situation, the Battalion Commander, Battalion Executive Officer, and the Battalion S3, all came by to see me. Seeing as it was probably the only time in my career I could get away with cussing out senior officers, I let fly with both barrels on each one as they came in to talk to me. Each one had ignored every warning sign, both overt and subtle, pushed me to my limit, pushed me past my limit, and then were "shocked" at what had happened.

*I was at rock bottom. When I got out of the hospital, I found out my unit had turned their back on me. The guys who were with me during the deployment reached out, but they were fewer and farther between than the new arrivals. Outside of those few I was a pariah. Phone calls and texts went unreturned. Greetings were ignored. Many wouldn't even look me in the eye. My Chain of Command was quick to distance themselves. However, despite treating me like a leper, my Chain of Command were quick to spread the story of how they had "tried everything they could" to help me... and spread the story they did...*

# Interlude:
# Victory Base Complex, Baghdad, Iraq
# January 2009 – January 2010

*One event started my ascent from rock bottom. An act of kindness saving my career and my life. A gesture of compassion so far past what I deserved. While I was in the hospital, my old boss walked in, saw me, and looked at my current Battalion Commander. With no hesitation he said three words I will never forget: "I'll take him."*

*This man saved my career. More importantly, he saved my life. Everyone else viewed me as a "problem" a "Serious Incident Report" and a "High Risk Soldier." He saw me as a person, an Officer, and a Soldier. While I felt worthless, he recognized my value as a human being, separating me as a person from my problems. He refused to let me pity myself and was always available to talk and listen when I needed. He helped put me back together, took me on as a protégé, and became my mentor. He guided me, taught me, pushed me to grow even when I thought I could not, and refused to coddle me.*

*At the time I was angry, furious even, with the Army, my old leadership, and how I'd been treated. This man reminded me why I joined and why I wanted to stay. When one set of Army leaders failed me, another Army leader refused to give up on me, refused to leave me behind, and refused to let me quit on myself. He rekindled my passion to serve and fed my determination to succeed. I would not be here today if it wasn't for him. Every day I strive to live up to the potential he saw in me and make him proud. I would not waste his faith in me. Even today we're still close and keep in touch.*

*I found a therapist off post who was an old Vietnam vet and understood what I struggled with. I made new friends in my new unit. I cut down my drinking and tossed out the easily abused pills the Army gave me. I still struggled with depression, but I no longer struggled with suicide. I was still a little wild and reckless in my personal* life, but I was getting it under control and taking active steps to change myself.

I wrote more and explored my feelings. I started doing things again: I went out to eat, saw movies, went to malls and shopped. Things were hard at first. I'd always had someone to do these things with before and it was strange doing them alone. Hell, it was downright depressing. The first time I went out to dinner alone I spent most of the time trying not to break down in tears. However, I found out I like my own company. I liked myself. I didn't need someone else to enjoy life. I could do things I enjoyed on my own. I kept myself moving, kept myself engaged with the outside world, and while it wasn't a magic solution, it helped ease the depression and sense of isolation. I even (briefly) dated someone again. I wasn't healthy by any means, but I made progress.

Many of the old scars from the first deployment remained and I still hadn't confronted them yet. Thinking of Rustamiyah still brought back too many painful memories. I still blamed myself for what happened on May 28, 2007. Some nights I still dreamt of blood and fire.

Still, I was making progress one day at a time.

I came home from my first deployment on January 22, 2008.

On January 21, 2009, a year to the day, I stepped back on a plane and headed back to Baghdad.

My second deployment was the polar opposite of the first. The easiest way to sum it up: the first was a combat tour, while the second was simply a deployment. The first time around I was in a line unit trying to survive a living charnel house. The second time around I was on staff *while living on one of the largest, and most secure places in Iraq: Victory Base Complex.*

*Known as the "Land of the Big PX" (due to the Costco sized PX that AAFES ran) VBC was as far from the war you could get while being in theater. It began as five separate camps that eventually grew together. We jokingly referred to it as "Fort Hood, Forward". I had my own F-150 I drove around when I was off. That's right, I had off time. VBC's size is hard to fathom, so I'll give two points of reference. First, it takes 2 hours to drive the drivable perimeter. I know because I did it all the time when I got bored, stressed, or couldn't sleep. Second, the indirect fire alarm didn't go off every time we got shelled because the place was so large mortars and rockets would often hit unoccupied areas.*

*I also had my choice of five chow halls to go to, some of which included delicacies like sliced, fresh mango and fucking quiche. If I didn't like the menu I could go to Burger King, Subway, Popeye's, Pizza Hut, or any of the other numerous local food joints. The haji shop doesn't have the bootleg you want? No problem, just drive to one of the seven others or visit the weekend bazar.*

*Seriously, the second deployment was a paid vacation compared to the first. Mostly, I did office work. As the Battalion Logistics Office it was my job to ensure our Battalion and attachments were properly supported. I spent a lot of time writing checks with the Army's money. While I wasn't kicking down doors, I learned a lot about a different side of the Army that would later influence my development as an Officer.*

*I patrolled a handful of times to visit outposts we supported, but this time I was along for the ride instead of leading the patrol. However, I remember one patrol in vivid detail: every site, sound, and sensation. It was the patrol to FOB Rustamiyah.*

## March 31, 2009: So Long, Rustamiyah

*Halfway down the road to Hell,*
*Betwixt the Sand and Fire,*
*Lays a place of blood, and wrath, and tears,*
*And we called it Rustamiyah*

Today. Today was..... Today. Today I attended the closing of FOB Rustamiyah, the FOB where I spent my first deployment. It was odd walking around. Everything was gone. Buildings empty. Trailers gone. A place that once held a large amount of American combat power seemed to sleep restlessly amidst the sand. I walked the FOB as I had done countless times before when I was-

*Hey! Did you guys do your debriefs after patrol?*

-here last time. The ceremony was typical. Speeches by our General. Speeches by the Iraqi Generals. Iraqis praising the sacrifices of American and Iraqi Soldiers who-

*Goddammit, leave the fucking vehicle! You can't get to him! The whole thing is on fire! He's gone, man!*

-gave their lives to provide the Iraqi military academy a new glorious beginning. The band plays. Iraqi cadets march forward to raise their flags. A bugler-

*Please rise for roll and taps. Baker! Here, Sergeant! Smalls! Here Sergeant! Christopher! ... SGT Christopher! ... SGT Caleb Christopher! .... Sergeant Major, SGT Christopher is not here with us tonight!*

-blows notes into the wind while the Colors snap in the breeze. As I walk, I see them. Hear them whisper. Ghosts. Friends, brothers, comrades, and soldiers, for whom Rusty was the last home they knew. I see scenes, happy and sad, played out, slow motion, thin and wispy, as the smoke rises from a lit cigarette. I walk to my old company area and-

*Hey, does anybody realize that even though we're all out here playing football, half of us are STILL running around with cigarettes dangling from the lips?*

-try the door open. Unlocked. Two mattresses on the floor. Empty wall lockers. A patch on the wall still there from the last time a rocket had-

*INCOMING!!! INCOMING!!! INCOMING!!!*

-slammed into it just before I had moved in. Farther back. Dillon lived here. Akers stayed there. Smoked a hookah with D22's crew right there. Played fetch with Reyes, the company dog, back there. Games of soccer and stickball in the quad. Juice walked out of that room one day wearing nothing but a cup and his helmet. Truck line-

*Is that a GOAT in my room? AND it's wearing my STETSON?!?!?!?! How- no WHERE in the HELL did you guys get a goat?*

-Over there. Figs room was there before-

*Hey, I'm from D CO. One of my Soldiers just came into your aid station from a sniper attack. His name was.... No, seriously.... You better go fucking check again, Sergeant! He was FINE when he got there 10 minutes ago! ...On the table? ...I ...thank you, Sergeant. ...Mustang Mike, Desperado Mike. Confirmed, one friendly KIA....*

-the sniper attack. CP where I used to come and watch crappy late night TV when I couldn't sleep. Mike Gulf's room where-

*Sir, I told you. No one can take me in Guitar Hero when it comes to 'Killing in the Name Of'!*

-countless hours spent playing Guitar Hero between patrols. Swing by the motor pool. Empty. The ground smoothed out, the dips, gouges, and ruts from tanks and Bradleys erased by time. Chief's office there. Ratchet was over there. Soaked in sweat while I broke track under spotlights right over there. Swing by the old battalion headquarters. Step into the TOC. Empty. Quiet now. I'm by myself, all-

*Mustang Mike, Desperado 5! Contact EFP! Three urgent WIA or possibly KIA, one tank destroyed and burning! I have two severe WIA and evac'ing them to Loyalty! The driver is still trapped and the tank is still burning. It's me and three others here with one working tank. I need any available US force to move to my position NOW! I am in TROUBLE!*

-alone. As I walk, the ghosts continue to whisper. One by one they leave until it's just me. Rustamiyah is gone, and with it go the ghosts and the shades of the last deployment. I get back to the truck line and suit up. I take one last drag, step into the truck, raise the ramp, and we take off. As we pull out the gate I look over my shoulder-

*Remember, we do this by the numbers. We go in, hit the building hard, snatch the target, and chuck deuces, same as we've done a hundred times before. We do as we're trained, and we'll all be back drinking near beer in no time.*

-And catch one last glimpse as Rustamiyah fades from my view for the last time.

*Sara and I attempted to patch things up during my second deployment (we were both on VBC), but what started hopeful ended with us not even being on speaking terms. It wasn't anyone's fault. There was just too much in the way, too much hanging between us.*

*Coming back from the second deployment was just as rough as the first. When I left, there was no one to see me off. I woke up in a hotel and took a cab to the headquarters. While people were saying final goodbyes to family and friends in the gym I sat alone listening to my iPod. When I came back my parents were there to greet me, but after a few days they went back home. I would see them in a couple weeks for leave. After leave, I'd get ready to leave Fort Hood for Fort Knox and the Maneuver Captain's Career Course.*

*The intervening time was hell. When I came home the first time, Sara was there to greet me. This time, when my parents left, I was alone. I started sleeping on the couch after Sara and I broke up and I still wouldn't sleep in my bed. The TV sort of helped the insomnia, and after sleeping next to someone for so long the bed just felt big, empty, and lonely.*

*All my friends from my unit were off with their own families. Instead of taking this time to examine my issues I filled the space with distractions. I drank and I partied from January of 2010 until I left for the Career Course once again choosing diversions from my pain instead of coping with it. I lied to myself that I was fine, having "fun" and "living life", but every night ended the same: alone in my apartment, drunk, and wondering why I kept going, wondering why no one loved me, and wondering if it would ever get better. I was terribly lonely, but fear of rejection and judgment kept me from forming any kind of meaningful connection.*

*Opening up was hard. Trusting was harder. Thankfully, I gained an incredible friend who helped me get through this period of my life. Without her influence I don't think I'd have stopped spiraling downward. We were both coming off of rough periods in our lives and understood each other. We could relate, listen to each other without judgment, and keep each other in check with tough love. Our ability to talk to each other openly and honestly regarding the things we went through and were struggling with were critical in helping each other through our problems. We became each other's support system, something that would continue when I went to Fort Knox and she went to law school nearby.*

*I left Fort Hood for Fort Knox in May of 2010. I took some much needed leave time on my way. Tried to sort my head out. Wrote a lot. Self-medicated with alcohol even more. I thought I was handling my problems, but I wasn't. I was still afraid to confront my feelings and problems. Alcohol had become my Band-Aid of choice. When I drank I didn't care, and if I didn't care then I didn't miss Sara, didn't smell Acker's burning flesh, and couldn't hear Peters begging me to not let him die. I wanted to drown my memories. I wanted to forget. I didn't realize that trying to cope with alcohol was a dead end. After a while, alcohol doesn't even numb the pain, but drinking has become the only thing you know how to do. I should have poured the liquor down the drain instead of down my throat.*

*While at the Career Course I went back to counseling. Our small group had a great bunch of guys, many whom had similar experiences during deployments. While it never turned into large scale group therapy we all shared one on one or in small groups. My instructor was also very supportive of me going to get help and even sat and talked with me a couple times. I began realizing I wasn't struggling alone. Many of us were carrying our burdens in silence. Still, while we shared in private, none of us were willing to talk in public, afraid of being branded with the stigmas associated with PTSD and depression*

*I tried dating a woman while at Knox, but it was more of the same. She wanted more than I did, and though I had feelings for her, they felt hollow and forced. I should have cared more. I WANTED to care more. It hurt that I couldn't. I felt broken. I couldn't understand what was wrong with me.*

*I don't know if I was moving backwards or forwards at that point. Memories from Rustamiyah still caused intense, emotional reactions. I still had nightmares. I still had insomnia. I still couldn't connect with people. It was a rollercoaster. Some days were good days. Some days were bad. Some days I felt ready to conquer the world and some days I could barely get out of bed. Still, I kept going, kept driving myself forward. Somewhere deep down I knew that if I stopped pushing then I wouldn't make it at all. I fought, I struggled, and I pulled myself along. I went to a lot of therapy. I slowly got better.*

*After the Career Course, I was assigned to a Cavalry Squadron in a Stryker Brigade. I made my way to Fort Lewis, which sits near Tacoma, WA, and reported in January 2011. I started my career as a tanker, but was interested in going to a Stryker unit to broaden my horizons and try something new. I was excited. It was a new Post and a new challenge. Most of all, it felt like a new start. To top it off, I would take command. I still remember the day I reported. I walked into the Squadron Commander's office and inwardly cheered when I saw he was wearing The Cav's combat patch.*

*During our talk his demeanor suddenly changes.*

*"Now, I'm just going to ask you this one time-"*

*Oh no.*

*"-and then we'll never mention it again."*

*Oh shit.*

*"I want you to tell me what happened with you at Fort Hood."*

*Suddenly my world was upended. Here I am, two and a half years, a successful deployment, two great OERs, a different division, different post, a different fucking CORPS for Christ's sake, and this comes up. How is this NOT behind me? Haven't I proven myself? What about my right to privacy?*

*It turns out that my name and the incident was spread amongst some of the senior officers in the Division. I also found out the Army had a loophole for sharing what should be protected medical information. When a soldier is designated as "high risk" the losing commander has to convey this information to the gaining commander, to include what factors and behaviors make the solider high risk. Any suicide attempt automatically designates a solider as high risk. The Army told me that my medical and mental health treatment is private. In the next breath it subsequently, by policy, violated my privacy. The Army told me and everyone else that it would get us help, it would protect our privacy, and any mental health issues or treatment would not affect our careers, yet the exact opposite of those things were staring me in the face.*

*So I told him what happened. I told him my story. My Commander thanked me for being honest. When I asked if this would affect me commanding a company he told me he didn't know. I walked out a little shaken, but felt confident that this was FINALLY behind me... until I got another slap in the face. The Army wanted me to do another mental health evaluation. That's right, three years and a deployment later the Army wanted to make sure I was "mentally fit" for my job. I went, inwardly seething the whole time, and passed the evaluation.*

*I worked in the S3 shop for a year and a half before I took command. I should have taken command much earlier than that and later found out that two factors caused the delay. First, the Troop Commander I would replace stayed on for part of the deployment until he had to leave for grad school.*

*The second was my suicide attempt.*

*Despite a successful deployment, two stellar OERs, and graduating from the Maneuver Captain's Career course on the Commandant's List, I still wore the scarlet letter of a High Risk Soldier. The High Risk Soldier designation was designed to make sure those soldiers received immediate, focused care and attention from Army medical, treatment, and counseling resources. Most of all, it was to guarantee the Chain of Command took a PROACTIVE role in ensuring these soldiers got help. Like many good ideas, it came from the best intentions. Like so many other good ideas it worked nothing like intended once put into practice.*

*The "High Risk" designation became a taint, a stigma, and a mark of shame. You were now "less than." It became a way to separate soldiers that commanders and leaders no longer wanted to deal with. It became a way to shove soldiers into a corner until they were discharged from the Army or left on their own. High Risk Soldiers certainly did not continue their careers. They were done. Even if you didn't get booted you could forget about getting the critical jobs that ensured advancement and promotion. This is why so many soldiers never sought help. If you answered the questions wrong (or were honest) you'd end up as "High Risk" and counting down the time until you got booted. Here's your discharge and don't let the door hit you in the ass on the way out. Go bother the VA.*

*The Army had labeled me a High Risk and that's all that mattered...*

*...But I was not about to let that stop me.*

# Afghanistan: Kandahar City, Kandahar, Afghanistan

## April 2012-January 2013

# Part VII:
# Back Into the Breach

When I arrived at Fort Lewis word was we would deploy to Afghanistan in the following year. We just didn't know when. I worked hard in the S3 shop trying to prove myself. Trying to prove (again) I was a valued asset, trying to prove (again) I was capable of deploying (even though I'd already done it four months after my suicide attempt), and I was ready for command.

Unfortunately, I fell back on old habits. My apartment was conveniently located within stumbling distance from a dive bar. I quickly became a regular, and not just an "I know what you're having" regular, but a "Please help bounce this guy from the bar" regular. It was also convenient in providing a string of unhealthy liaisons, the exact type of relationships I wanted to move away from. After five months of drowning myself in cheap drinks and random women I had an epiphany.

Ok, it was less of an epiphany and more of a serious system shock. I woke up from a hard night of partying, walked into my bathroom, and when I looked into the mirror I had no idea who was looking back at me. What the fuck was I doing and who was I turning into? Alcohol didn't solve my problems. I may be distracted when I got drunk, it may mask the pain, but when I sobered up my problems were still right in front of me along with a hangover and a lighter wallet. Partying and women didn't fix anything either. Once again, they were just things to distract me from my actual issues, not fix them. All those things were surface deep, just ways for me to run from what needed confronting.

Around May of 2011 I made a serious life change. I was tired of spending the majority of my time and money partying and drinking, realizing it was a poor substitute for my loneliness and problems. I decided to address them head on. I slowed my pace down, stopped chasing women, *and started focusing on becoming comfortable with myself once again.*

*When Sara left I felt unlovable, and that was a huge blow to my self-esteem. As a result, I often sought validation in female attention. That drove much of the partying I did, the random one night stands, and the revolving door of women who came in and out of my life. I was determined to learn to love myself again, to build my self-esteem, and be dependent on ME and no one else. No one else would determine my value. I was good enough for me, and that's what mattered. Slowly but surely my sense of self-worth came back.*

*Shortly after this realization a friend dragged me along to hang out with some guys from the unit. I didn't want to go, but I was bored and couldn't think of a good excuse to get out of it. By sheer chance, my future wife was also cajoled into going to the same party by one of her friends. We met at a friend's apartment and bonded over being the oldest people there. Two days later, on May 26, 2011, Lauren and I had our first date.*

*Something clicked. For the first time in years I could open up and form a meaningful, healthy relationship. Meeting Lauren was eye opening. It forced me to face my relationship fears and provided an impetus to, quite simply, get my shit together. I was terrified of screwing it up, but I had a reason to push past the fear. She was worth it. For the first time in years I gave a relationship an honest try. I didn't hold back. I had to trust at some point, so why not with her? If the relationship failed that would suck, but it didn't mean I was worthless. I loved me for me. Now I could love someone else.*

*When I wasn't spending time with Lauren I worked like a man possessed. I burned with determination to prove myself and rebuild my reputation. It didn't take long. My S3 recognized my potential and talent and actively mentored me. Before long I had gone from his assistant to his deputy, often running the staff when he and the XO had to handle other business. My performance caught the eye of other leaders around the Brigade. I was seen as incredibly smart, efficient, and able to work above my pay grade... and slightly flippant and needing maturity. Hey, like I said before, I'm not perfect... and I'm a bit of smartass.*

*In the fall we went to NTC and got the official word of our impending deployment. We would deploy in April of 2012 to Kandahar Province, Afghanistan. In January I decided that I wouldn't let opportunity pass me by and proposed. I was good with a long, open ended engagement, but Lauren broke me down into setting a date: May 26, 2013, the two year anniversary of our first date.*

*In early April, I called one of my old bosses, the man who saved my career and became my mentor, to talk about the upcoming deployment. We were going to Kandahar City where he had been in and around the area the past year. He told me, straight up, that it could be bad. Kandahar was highly contested and all the signs pointed to the same level of violence we had seen back in Baghdad in 2007. My blood froze. I was scared. Could I do that again? Go through that again? My life was just coming together.*

*The deployment came entirely too soon. I spent my last night lying in bed with my fiancée, her head on one shoulder and our dogs curled up on either side, thinking how I was the luckiest man in the world. My depression was in check, I felt confident, I had a woman who loved me, I was getting married when I got back, I would take command soon (AND I would get to do it in combat)...*

*everything seemed right with the world... and I was fearful the deployment would ruin it all.*

*I was terrified.*

*I was scared of failing. I was afraid that I would break down in combat, that I wouldn't be able to handle it. I was afraid of coming back crazy again. I was afraid of finally finding a woman I truly loved, only to miss out on life together because I died or came back wounded or crazy.*

*On April 28, 2012, I stepped on a plane, fear and all, and began my journey to Kandahar City, Afghanistan.*

*I still don't know how I forced myself onto that plane.*

### Email: April 30, 2012

We left Fort Lewis on Saturday and it was surprisingly hard. This is my third deployment. Trust me when I say this rodeo is getting old. The flight wasn't too bad, though I'm pretty sure I traveled forward in time as I left on a Saturday night and landed on a Monday morning after only 20 odd hours of flying. My body is still convinced it's lost a day somewhere and decided to make me pay for it by throwing a tantrum. Currently, I'm sitting at Manas AFB, Kyrgyzstan. Nothing like waking up after traveling for a day and you first thought is "Now just where the hell AM I?" Not going to lie, don't ask me to point to Kyrgyzstan on a map. I have no clue and don't want to embarrass myself. The Airmen who greeted us described it as "Someplace sandwiched between Asia and Europe where everyone chain smokes and you have the vague impression the locals are swearing at you in Russian while they smile." One cool thing is that you can see a massive mountain range off in the distance. It helps to block out the smell of diesel and sewage. We should be here one more day before heading to Kandahar Airfield (KAF) and the true start of the deployment. One day down, 269 to go...

Leading up to this deployment I had been struggling with a lot of emotions. It took me awhile to pin it down, but after a while, it came to me. I was afraid.
I was afraid, truly afraid. That was a new sensation for me. I can't recall a time in my life where I'd been afraid. Nervous? Sure. Anxious? Of course. The twitchy anticipation of the unknown? Definitely.... but never true fear. Never the cold, icy knot that grows in your belly, threatening to rob you of your senses and freeze your legs. I've never felt that before.

I narrowed it down to two reasons. First, I'm going back to combat. My first tour I was young and stupid, with zero knowledge of what I was getting into. I did not understand what combat was like. I was an Armor Officer, Tank Platoon Leader, trigger puller, and a 100% homegrown, Grade A, American Badass who would hunt down the enemy and win the war on my own with the blinding power of enthusiasm and American sunshine! I had no idea what it felt like to be blown up, have bullets whiz by my head, to see your brothers hurt, broken, and bleeding next to you. I had no idea what it was like to kill. I had no idea what it was like to come home to nightmares and insomnia, to chasing therapy sessions with liquor and the pills they fed you, and to see your relationship die slowly and painfully. I did not understand what it was like to watch your world, your life fall apart before your eyes and feel powerless to stop it. Now I know. I wish and pray that I NEVER again have to experience combat, to see my world in shades of fire and blood... This time I know the whole cost... and I am afraid.

    The second reason is that I actually have something to lose. When I went to Iraq the first time I came home to a girlfriend. This time I'm coming home to the woman who will soon be my wife. The thought of missing the chance to build a life with her, whether through death, injury, or emotional trauma, frightens me more than combat does. When I was a young Platoon Leader all I wanted to do was be Billy Badass, rip and run through Baghdad, and come home with my Combat Action Badge. I wanted to be a Battalion Commander, Brigade Commander, and, eventually, a General. Being a Soldier was the single most important thing in my world. It was how I defined myself. It was identity, ambitions, and aspirations. What do I want now? I want to hold my wife, be a husband and a father, and start a family. Being a Soldier still defines me, but it isn't the be all, end all it once was. As much as I want to be a Soldier, I want to be a good man even more.

I once had an old NCO tell me that courage isn't being unafraid, but being scared shitless and doing what needs doing anyway. There's no courage without fear. I'm no longer terrified. There's still fear, but it's changed to the healthy nervousness that anyone going into danger experiences, the kind that keeps you sharp and ready, the kind that keeps you alive. The fear is still there somewhere, but it's pushed aside in favor of what needs to be done. As far as combat goes, I'll do what needs to be done. I'll hunt down, close with, and teach the enemy the hard cost of trying to fight an American Soldier. I won't hesitate, falter, or fail.... I'll just be a little older and wiser while I do it. As far as my girl, well that one is simple. I'm coming home to my baby. Come hell or high water, I'm coming home.

**Email: May 8, 2012**

MAJ: Welcome to Camp Nathan Smith, CPT Wharton.

Me: Thank you sir, it's good to finally be-

MAJ: Good, now that you're here, I need you to start banging out these CONOPs and I need the first one in about three hours.

Me: Uh…ok…. What about transitioning with my counterpart?

MAJ: Yeah, yeah, yeah, you'll get to that.

Me: I also don't have any user accounts or a laptop ye-

MAJ: Negligible details.

Me: Well, can I at least go drop my bags in my room?

MAJ: Why? We set you up a cot right by your desk that way you can work as long as possible.

Me: Gee.... Thanks....

Ok, so the last part is a little exaggerated, but within 30 minutes of arriving to CNS (Camp Nathan Smith, the FOB I'm at) I was thrown to the bench, lashed to my oar, and set back to rowing. The first thing that hit me on arrival was that this was definitely NOT Iraq in a lot of ways.

First, Iraq had this magical thing called infrastructure. By the time we left, several FOBs, like Taji, Anaconda, and VBC resembled small cities. We used to joke that Camp Victory was nothing more than Fort Hood, Iraq. Even my first FOB, Rustamiyah, which was no paradise by any means, was much more developed than this. We've been in Afghanistan since 2001, and while KAF grew (and, like Camp Victory, seems to have forgotten there's a war going on), let's just say CNS leaves a lot to be desired. I don't know where all the money went, but it definitely skipped CNS. We still have guys living in tents. Not as transient, but permanently... And there's a Brigade Headquarters here.

Second, when I got to Iraq I got my battle space, my mission, and except for minor tweaks, that's what we did for the entire time. Not so much here. It seems like every now and then the powers that be in Afghanistan like to gather up all the pieces, throw them in the air, and scramble them around based on where they fall. From what I've seen and heard it isn't uncommon to pack up whole units and move them around the battle space (or sometimes regions), multiple times during a deployment.

Third, we've also encountered the ugly politics of combat. A counterinsurgency takes time to execute properly. You can't kill your way out. You "win" when the host nation government can sustain itself politically, economically, and militarily. The key is that they have to do it on their own. It's better to for them to do something tolerably than you to do it perfectly, but we're still playing to the old statistics. How many times have you cleared this area, how many times did you use this asset, how much money did you pump into local projects... We're slaves to statistics. So far my favorite is the named operation the Division executes that my Squadron is part of... When essentially our "part" is just doing our daily patrols. Nothing special. Nothing sexy. Why? It allows Division to say they've conducted X operation X number of times. So while the guys on the ground do what they always do, staffs burn through enormous amounts of man-hours and resources making orders, publishing products, and killing trees to churn stuff out that's no more than a prettied up version of daily business... Yeah... Winning the war one bureaucratic maneuver at a time....

Why? Essentially it comes down to who butters your bread and what have you done for me lately. This is not a conventional fight anymore. Division and Brigade Commanders aren't maneuvering large formations around the field, coordinating effects and massing fire power. This is a street fight. It's Squad Leaders, Platoon Leaders, and Company Commanders partnering with Afghans and moving the ball forward through personal relationships and a lot of hard work. Yes, the Colonels and the Generals work with their Afghan Generals counterparts. Yes, we do need strategic frameworks, campaign plans, etc, etc, etc. I'm not saying none of that is important. What I am saying is the war isn't being "won" or "lost" in the operation centers or conference rooms anymore. It's being won or lost by that American and Afghan Private standing guard together, by a Platoon Leader working with a local Checkpoint Commander, and by a Company Commander working with an Afghan Company Commander on how Afghan Forces can disrupt local terror networks.

Still, Army culture is one of "what have you done for me lately?" We haven't truly (and I daresay our military culture makes it almost IMPOSSIBLE) let someone else take the lead. We don't do well accepting half-assed results from our partners and, with each other, we don't accept less than our own standards. Come evaluation time, "What have you done for me lately? What are your stats? How many missions have you accomplished?" and the other measurable tangibles matter more than how TRULY effective you've been in professionalizing the local Afghan Forces. The current model drives conducting 100 missions with Afghans where they do little more than stay in their trucks, simply walk the streets, and follow our lead. I'd argue that 20 missions that start with the Afghans not knowing which way was up and progress to where they can plan, execute, and command the operations themselves do more to contribute to our long term goal. However, 100 reads a hell of a lot better than 20 come evaluation time. Are all higher commanders fixed in this mindset? No, but our Army culture is, and going against your culture is very hard indeed.

Other than that, things haven't been too bad. Despite working in a wooden box inside an old cannery (they built wooden office "buildings" inside an abandoned factory) things aren't too bad and I can't complain. The gym is in the same building so it's easy to sneak away. We've nicknamed the gym the "Prison Yard" and fully expect a shanking in the next day or two. I'll send pictures when I can. You have to see it to believe it.

Our "PX" here is a small room with wooden shelves. Our veritable Wal-Mart provides a wide ranging plethora of options, and I don't know how I manage to decide between ice tea, canned tuna, Clorox bleach, or Tostitos salsa. Pretty slim pickings. Keurig K-Cups, drink mix, canned fruit, jerky, toiletries, etc. are always appreciated. Whatever we don't use personally always goes into the communal pot, so anything helps out somebody. Lastly, thank you for all the encouragement and responses so far. I'm sorry I haven't been able to write back individually, but I will. I still don't have an unclassified laptop in the office yet and I'm barely in my room. Till next time.

### Email: May 12, 2012

Finally got a decent internet connection, so I'll be able to write and respond more. The train keeps moving faster and faster here. Time does weird things during deployment. There's always more work than hours in the day. I've only been at the FOB for 10 days, but it feels like weeks. The days of the week run together, dissolving in a haze of bloodshot eyes, too much coffee, and not enough sleep. You're never quite sure if you made that call, passed on the last order, or whether you meant to task this unit or the other. It's all one big blur.

The same blur covers the States, where people have tuned out and forgotten about the war. A classmate of mine is a Company Commander for a Rifle Company in one of our sister battalions. He's out west in Maiwand. In two days, he lost-

*-CONTACT EFP, RTE Brewers! I have a tank on fire and three urgent surgi-*

-several of his soldiers. Multiple wounded in an IED strike one day, with two of them having to be evacuated to Germany. The day after his company got hit again, with-

*-Where's the sniper at? Check that window! We have a man down! Grab the med- Holy shit, it's Figgy! Somebody get-*

-one soldier killed and another gravely wounded. More than 1,500 Soldiers, Sailors, Airmen, and Marines have given their lives in-

*Mom, that isn't funny. What do you mean Neale's-*

-Afghanistan. More than 15,000 wounded. It's easy to forget what each of those numbers represents. Back home we see and experience the war in glimpses and snatches. A report here. A snippet on the news there. A good news story about someone-

*-Christopher! SSG Christopher! SSG Caleb Christopher! 1SG, SSG Christopher is not here tonight-*

-coming home. It's easy to forget that behind each of those numbers exists a person. A soldier not coming home. Children left without a parent. A parent burying their child. Brothers and sisters saying goodbye. And it doesn't stop at that. It's a family coping with someone severely disabled. It's learning how to bathe your spouse when they no longer have legs to stand in the shower. It's a Soldier in therapy because while he never feared bombs and bullets, he's terrified of losing his wife and family because he can't reconnect. It's easy to forget the human-

*-Sir, sir, please, God, don't let me die, sir, I don't want to die sir, don't let me die, I want to see my little girl, oh God, I'm dying, don't let me die-*

-cost and what that all means. The war still goes on. Whether you agree or disagree, I don't care. It's irrelevant. What matters is never forgetting that for every number we see, every article we read, and every story we hear, represents a person. Represents a life. We don't want your pity. We don't want your thanks. We just don't want to be forgotten.

### Email: May 22, 2012

People always ask what combat and deployments are like. I'll tell you. Deployments are boring as hell. Most people think deployment equals to combat. During my first deployment, which definitely included combat, I can count roughly eight times where people enthusiastically tried to kill me and vice versa... in 15 months. This doesn't count the mortar attacks, car chases, random stray shots, etc. Eight times in 15 months. Not exactly a lot (although a bullet zipping by even once is one time too many), but about average for most of us then, and we were in a fairly kinetic area. The second time I went to Iraq, it was definitely a deployment instead of a combat tour. I remember being mortared/rocketed about six to eight times all year with only two coming relatively close (I was asleep in my trailer when a rocket hit the barrier next to it). Mostly, it was office work: contract work, keeping the Battalion's books straight, and spending the government's money.

Most of deployment is mind numbing repetition and trying to find ways to keep from clawing out your eyes as a result. I haven't been deployed a month yet and I want to drive spikes into my eyes. Now to be fair, I'd rather be bored than shot at, but this isn't the boredom of not being able to travel or see a movie or even go out to dinner once in a while. This is the boredom of literally doing the exact same thing every day. Wake up, sit at desk, work on orders, memos, and PowerPoint for 12-14 hours, go to gym at some point, go to bed, repeat. Every ...single ...goddamn ...day. Unlike my last deployment, where at least the office had a bit of variety, I work the same thing, the same issues, the same problems day in and day out. It is driving me up the wall. The other day I just got up and walked the entire camp just to vary the routine. Still, I can't complain. I have working internet, three hots, a bed (WITH actual mattress), working showers, and a gym that, while looking like it came out of the yard at San Quentin, is pretty functional.

On a side note, I've run into a couple classmates and old friends since I arrived. One is with an advisory team that worked a prisoner transfer with us. Another friend, who was a Company XO in my last unit, is with the outgoing brigade as a Battle Captain (trust me, the job isn't anywhere NEAR as sexy as it sounds...). A third is an MP Company Commander who works next door. It's kind of odd running into people you haven't seen in years. It always seems you freeze people in your mind at the last moment you saw them. For me and the MP it was kind of a shock. She'd hardened more than I ever could imagine. I was no longer the chain smoking, tequila swilling, womanizer I had been when she last knew me. It was almost like meeting again for the first time. It's funny how much time and life grows and changes people. I barely recognize some classmates anymore. Others I've grown closer to as adults then we were as children playing at war.

We're barely in (or at) our collective 30s and most of us have deployed multiple times, seen and lead Soldiers in combat, and had friends, peers, and our soldiers die before their time. Does that make us old? I don't know. I know I've lived a lot of life for just shy of 29. I know that the person I was at 18, 19, hell, even 25, wouldn't recognize me now. The last memory I had of my classmate across the hall was from and assignment the summer before our senior year. We were sitting on the steps of a barracks in Fort Carson, CO with three other classmates, passing around a bottle of SoCo and talking about how we will finally be Firsties. Now, she's an experienced company commander. She's married. She's a grown woman. I'm about to take command. I'm about to get married (yeah, I know, I still can't believe it sometimes either). I've grown into a man. I've seen joy and pain. Had triumph and tragedy. Watched my life fall apart and somehow, by the grace of God, put it back together. It's funny how far we come, and it's funnier how seldom we realize it.

**Email: May 28, 2012**

*"Halfway down the trail to Hell,*
*In a shady meadow green*
*Are the Souls of all dead troopers camped,*
*Near a good old-time canteen.*
*And this eternal resting place*
*Is known as Fiddler's Green."*
-From Fiddler's Green, an old Cavalryman's poem

*"May it be said 'Well done. Be thou at peace'"*
-United States Military Academy, "The Alma Mater"

      I first met Neale Shank when I joined JROTC my freshman year of high school. I remember thinking how tough he was, how strong, how he had it all figured out and how he seemed to just…well…know. Neale took me under his wing back then. Taught me the basics. Showed me the ropes. Got me into drill team, Adventure Training, taught me how to spin a rifle without cracking my head open or breaking a finger. I remember Neale joining the Army when he graduated from Concordia and I couldn't help but think that I'd want to do that someday. I graduated, went to West Point, and found out that he would be my classmate. I was so excited. I remember seeing Neale here and there during basic, and he always shot me a glance, gave me a nod, or told me to hang tough. We went through the academy with different crowds, but I still remember lots of shared plane rides home and even more shared beers down in the Firstie Club. I remember branch night and Neale, who had gone infantry, giving me shit about how I would get fat and lazy for becoming a tanker. I remember deploying that first time and Neale telling me I'd be fine as a Platoon Leader. I remember a day in Iraq like any other, sitting out in front of my hooch, smoking another countless cigarette when my mom called and told me that Neale was gone. I've seen a lot of death in my life to this point, some of them very horrible and violent, but none has hit me like that one.

    I remember talking to Tom Martin over instant messenger that first deployment. Talking about being Platoon Leaders, about the fight in our sectors. Taking Tom's advice to try to stay positive and see the good. I remember thinking how much I looked up to him, how I wished I was as good of a soldier as him, as good of a man as he was. I remember talking to him the morning of the day he died. He was supposed to be waiting on his flight home. He was supposed to be going home to marry Angela and start a life with her. Instead, he told me he was going on one last patrol, one last time showing the new unit how the sector ran, because if he didn't then who would? He may show them something that last patrol that may save a life… and when the Iraqi sprayed the patrol with a burst of gunfire Tom was the only one hit.

I remember the Mustangs who made Rustamiyah their final home... Fig, Harper, Christopher, and many others. I remember Emily Perez, another classmate of mine, killed in 2006, the first of us to die, when her vehicle was hit by an IED. She was on her way to help run a medical clinic for Iraqis. And now, my Brigade will remember the six soldiers who have given their lives since we took over three weeks ago. And it isn't just this war. We remember all those who have gone before us. The men who stormed the beaches at Normandy, froze in Korea, sweltered in the jungles of Vietnam, jumped into Panama, rolled thunder through Kuwait to Iraq the first time, walked the streets of Iraq the second, and hunted Taliban and Haqqani through the mountains in Afghanistan. To all of those whose final home was hundreds or thousands miles away, whose final embrace was a brother holding them in their final moments, and who gave their last in service for their country, we say thank you. You will not be forgotten. You will be remembered.

Take a moment over Memorial Day and say a prayer for the families of those who gave their all.


**Email: June 1, 2012**

When I was in Iraq, I was always aghast at the level of corruption. Cops shaking down the locals. Terrorists getting released in spite of overwhelming evidence because they knew somebody... or their money did. I once saw a local man we gave MREs to (after he begged us to help him feed his starving family) selling what we gave him the next day. It was Shia against Sunni, Maliki against Mooqi (what we called Muqtada al-Sadr), and everybody trying to get over on somebody else. Still, I believed what I saw was the result of war, poverty, and trying to seek some semblance of a life out of the situation. When your world shrinks to survival a lot of moral qualms tend to go by the wayside.

Afghanistan feels different. The corruption here seems less a result of the situation and more cultural... which begs the question: If it's culture, is it corruption? If it's "custom" to show appreciation for your promotion by giving your boss a "gift" then is it wrong? You're not paying bribes to police, you're paying a toll, and if you can't pay, then police aren't robbing you as they are taking the toll from the goods you're carrying. Better yet, we detained a guy based on mountains of evidence at the scene plus statements from elders and neighbors regarding his activities. In less than a day he was released because he's a "friend" of the country's President. Does it matter if that friendship sprung from a one time "donation" to a mutual acquaintance? Friendship is friendship, right?

I was talking with a friend the other night and we concluded that in Afghanistan you aren't backing the "good guy" as much as you're picking which criminal you want to get in bed with. We pour money and resources by the billion and blood by the gallon which the Afghan government happily accept in private but bluster and shout in public. They're sovereign, independent, and we must respect and accept their wishes.

However, down at the patrol level, on the street and up in the mountains, the Afghans tell a different story. Afghan Police at our outposts won't sit in the guard towers because it's hot and it's boring... And they can't smoke hash up there. They want us to pull tower guard for them. We go to them and ask them what their patrol plan is and they defer to us... yet get mad when we ask them to do something they don't want to do. They abandon guard positions at the base entrances at night so they can go smoke hash or they fall asleep because they know we'll fill in since we take security seriously. They will loudly proclaim how this is their country and how they fight for it daily. In the same breath they then tell us they will quit and stop fighting when we leave because the Taliban will come back, kill them, and take over again.

We also recently had a rather powerful figure in the Kandahar City security hierarchy jerk around and disrespect our Squadron Commander. He wanted a new checkpoint built and when we asked him what the Afghan plan for it was, he essentially challenged my boss's pride, saying he didn't think we could produce.... So now we're building the checkpoint for him... after he backed out of the site recon with my boss because he had "better things to do".... And then moving the checkpoint site miles from where we planned it... all at the last minute. And why do we do it? Because we "need" our Afghan "partners" to get things done. We need to help, assist, and put them in the lead, but never do it for them... unless it comes to politics and influence.

I'm not saying that all Afghan politicians, police, or soldiers are like this, but I see enough to be disturbing. There are still the true believers. The ones who truly want to fight the Taliban, are sick of the corruption, and want to do it themselves because it's THEIR country, not an American objective. Still, like good men anywhere they are few and far between.

How do you keep soldiers believing when the writing isn't just on the wall, but your country's leaders and other world leader have declared endgame and set a date? More so, how do you explain this to the widows, fathers, sisters, mothers, and brothers of those killed in these final days? This is what we deal with day to day. These are the challenges bouncing around my head as command gets closer. We'll figure it out. We have to. We won't let this all be for nothing.

**Email: June 18, 2012**

Not much has been going on here lately. In fact, it's been downright slow. Fine with me. However, a lot of that is about to change. It's time for the great job shuffle. Platoon Leaders are becoming XOs, XOs are moving up to staff, and the staff captains are preparing to move to different staff jobs or take command of Troops... like me.

In about a month to a month and a half I will head down to B Troop and begin change of command inventories and transition. I'll get a month to pick the outgoing commander's brain, make sure all the property is squared away, and prepare to take over and execute my mission. Command is what all officers live for. You're it. You're the boss. You're in charge. You get the incredible privilege of leading Soldiers, shaping lives, and doing some good. It's an incredible responsibility. I believe most refer to it as a "joyous burden." The transition is incredibly important as the outgoing commander can give you good advice, set you up for success, and get you started on the right path. The incoming-outgoing commander relationship is crucial during the transition. And the guy I'm replacing hates me.

I'll call him John for ease of reference. John and I never saw eye to eye and even had into a few arguments in the past. In one instance a year ago (one I'm not proud of), a phone call ended with me cussing John out and hanging up on him. What he did doesn't matter. I should have been more mature than I acted. I apologized to John and resolved to myself to be a professional, regardless of his actions, and I have. I thought we had moved past that and we had at least come to where we could work together professionally, even if we disliked each other, and all this time it seemed like we had. And then I found out he was trying to sabotage me and keep me from command.

Thankfully, the words he was placing in the ears of my boss and my boss's boss went unheeded. I'm still set to take command. I had a long talk with the chaplain today about the whole situation and he told me some great advice. He told me regardless of what happens during the transition I will take command at the end of that month. The second thing he told me is that all eyes will be on me to see how I react, and how I react will set the tone for my command and my soldiers' perception of me. In other words, kill him with kindness. I've resolved to do that, and God knows I've prayed for the strength. I've waited too long, overcome too much, and worked too hard to let one jackass screw it all up by allowing him to dictate my emotions and responses.

So I'm waiting patiently, studying, working out, preparing. This is my chance to do good. I don't mean doing "good" in the sense of mission accomplishment. That goes without saying. I mean doing "good" in the sense of influencing a soldier's life for the better, of running an organization soldiers are proud to be a part of, of having a young soldier or Platoon Leader saying "That's my Commander. I want to be like him one day." Most importantly, once we get back I want to be able to help soldiers avoid going through what I went through after my first deployment. If I can save just ONE person from that then I can rest easy. It isn't about me. I don't care about my own evaluation. It's about the men who will be my soldiers. Command is almost here and I can't wait.

## Email: June 21, 2012

*Turn left halfway down to hell,*
*And cross the mountains far,*
*A place where foes and friends are one,*
*And we named it Kandahar*

**Destroy:** A tactical mission task that physically renders an enemy force combat-ineffective until it is reconstituted.

Two dead.

It could have been worse.

11 wounded with nine evacuated out of theater for good. We got lucky.

The guys at that outpost started that day like any other. The boss doing PT with his Afghan police counterpart. Some guys still in the rack. Some guys counting down till the end of their guard shift. Just another Army morning.

And then the gunmen opened fire. He wasn't a random Afghan, but an Afghan we worked with, trained with, and knew by face and name walked the shooters through security. One Afghan commander died first, gunned down in his bed, the other out with our guys doing PT. When they saw his room was empty, they headed for our tents instead.

As I walked into the Squadron TOC that morning all hell was breaking loose. By the time things got sorted out and under control an American and one of our Afghan interpreters were dead. The American was the Squadron's Law Enforcement Professional. These guys are civilian cops from the States who volunteered to come over and help train Afghan police. This was his fourth trip between Iraq and Afghanistan. 11 of our Soldiers lay wounded, several in critical condition, with an equal number of Afghan police killed and wounded.

And we were lucky.

You've heard about this in the news before: "Green on Blue." Green on Blue is a situation where host nation forces engage U.S. or Coalition forces. Often the reports talk about how it's caused by U.S. Soldiers being culturally insensitive, by disrespecting their culture, besmirching their honor, or as revenge for crimes real or imaginary. Sometimes that's true. But not all. And not most.

It's one thing when the enemy blends in with crowd of civilians. It's another thing when he's standing next to you, weapon in hand, trained by you, and inside a place where you're supposed to be safe. Every day we're told that "closer is safer." Live with the Afghans, train with them, eat with them, sleep next to them, bring them close to you, form relationships with them, and this will keep you safe. Typically it's true. Unfortunately, when it isn't true the results are devastating. It's worse than getting shot at during patrol or blown up by a random roadside bomb. It isn't faceless. It isn't impersonal. It was Hakim, the guy you swapped smokes with while on guard. It was Abdulla, the one you played soccer with. It wasn't faceless. It was betrayal.

And it plays hell with Soldiers. How do you trust the guy walking behind you on patrol with a loaded automatic rifle when "one of them" just gunned down 13 of your brothers? How do you train the guys when "they" just attacked us? How do you keep them as Hakim and Abdulla instead of turning them into "fucking hadjis"? We ask our Soldiers to do incredible things every day and we often take it for granted. These attacks make a leader's job that much harder. How do you trust your friends when they may kill you at any moment?

Well, how do you?

## **Email: July 14, 2012**

"My idea is that every specific body strives to become master over all space and to extend its force (its will to power) and to thrust back all that resists its extension. But it continually encounters similar efforts on the part of other bodies and ends by coming to an arrangement ("union") with those of them that are sufficiently related to it: thus they then conspire together for power. And the process goes on." -Friedrich Nietzsche

"What is good? All that heightens the feeling of power in man, the will to power, power itself. What is bad? All that is born of weakness. What is happiness? The feeling that power is growing, that resistance is overcome." -Friedrich Nietzsche

Finally.

It's finally here.

After all the waiting, preparing, training, struggle, and sacrifice it's finally here. Tomorrow I head out to start my transition into command. Words can't express how excited I am. The only other time I've ever been this excited was graduation day at West Point. Same mixture of excitement, nervous, and a bit of trepidation. It will take about two weeks to transition between property inventories, learning the area, meeting everyone, and integrating into the Troop. No, not THE Troop... MY Troop. MY Troop... MY Soldiers... MY command...

I've taken a hard look at myself the last couple of weeks. I've done a lot of talking with the other Troop Commanders, my Squadron Commander, my S3 (who has become another mentor), and others. I've read, observed, and listened. The overwhelming conclusion I've seen and heard is command is both a tremendous rush and a tremendous burden. A rush from the sense of being in charge, of being able to chart the course for you unit. A burden of responsibility and nagging wonder if there was something you could have done better.

Command is power and authority coupled with tremendous responsibility. Unfortunately, I've watched many a commander become infatuated with the power and forget the responsibility. Power, in any form, is always a dangerous thing, and when you have the power accompanying command it can be dangerous. I've watched my brothers here take command and seen the best and worst of their personalities magnified hundred fold, their traits brought to the surface and amplified. I've seen them build their men up and I've seen them dispatch men on petty tasks for their own personal comfort. I've seen them working on their vehicles in the heat with their men and I've seen them yell at a junior soldier for their not refilling their personal stash of sugar and creamer. I've seen them give their soldiers socks and t-shirts from their own clothing and I've watched them force their XO's to make shady and borderline illegal purchases just so they could have the latest and greatest gear for themselves.

Everyone always gets the quote wrong. "Power corrupts and absolute power corrupts absolutely." The correct wording is "power *tends* to corrupt and absolute power corrupt absolutely." Everyone says you can judge a man's character by what he does when no one's looking. As revealing, and often forgotten, is what a man does when given power. Does he use it to enhance the lives of others or himself? Does he belong to his men, or do his men belong to him? Does it bring out the best in him, and, by extension, those around him, or does it bring out the worst?

This is the first time in my life I will experience that kind of power and influence.

And I worry.

What kind of man will it make me? What will it reveal about me? Will I TRULY be able to live and practice the leadership principles I've studied and espoused, or will I give in to pressures from my bosses, exhaustion, and frustration and become something I hate? A friend I told this to told me I shouldn't worry about it. Just the fact I was worried about how I'd react showed I had a good enough heart NOT to become what I hated. Still, I don't think it's that easy. It's never the big things at first. Corruption always starts small. The slope is gradual and slippery, the "rewards" often tangible and seductive, and the outcomes generally fall in your favor. If you don't believe me, check out the studies showing how many military, corporate, and business leaders rate fairly high on a scale of sociopathy. Actually, you don't even need to do that. Just look around at how many leaders in our own society clawed their way to the top by violating ethics and propelling themselves forward at the expense of others.

And they made it to the top.

And often stay there.

If it's so easy, why worry about doing the right thing? It's there in front of you and all you have to do is reach out and grab it. At end of the day, I guess it's just a simple mathematical equation. What's worth more to you? Power? Or your soul?

In about two weeks I'll be in command officially. I can't help feeling this is the first step of something I can't even imagine.

# Part VIII: Command

*It was finally here.*

*After all this time waiting, struggling, proving and re-proving myself, I would take command. Words couldn't describe how happy and excited I was. Not only was I taking command, I would command in combat. This was IT! This is what every officer waits and trains for.*

*Command.*

*I would be working with Afghan Police and government officials, something I had been looking forward to. I would be on my own COP with a large degree of autonomy. This was it.*

*The Squadron would soon transition missions from active partnership with the Afghans to more of an over watch role. That also meant we would get to execute other missions across the Brigade battle space as required. A platoon here for a week, an air assault there; we didn't know what to expect, but it would be good to get into the fight. However, my Troop was in a unique situation. Before the change of mission I had three outposts, three reconnaissance platoons, a military police platoon, a headquarters, and my fires platoon. After the transition, we closed two platoon outposts, the MPs went back to their parent company, and one of my recce platoons went up north to reinforce one of my sister companies.*

*I was now the only Troop in the Squadron that still manned its own COP and responsible for over watching all of western Kandahar City. I was also short a platoon. While it may sound like we drew the short straw, it was entirely the opposite. We loved it. Yes, it was rough. Yes, we were stretched thin. Still, we were on our own and putting in work. Also, due to our unique situation, we could keep close ties with a lot of the Afghans we had been working with.*

*I was commanding in combat.*

*Best of all, things were improving in tangible ways. The AUP in our area still needed a lot of help when I took over. A couple months into my command they called us less and less, had security under control to a large degree, and, minus some logistic aspects, started running the show themselves. It was night and day from Baghdad. Instead of watching my sector descend into blood and chaos, I saw it becoming a little better day by day.*

*I was becoming a believer.*

### Email: August 1, 2012

After all this time waiting, pushing, and fighting, I'm finally in command.

How do I feel? Thankful.

For those of you who know my whole story, it is an amazing testament to God's awesome, enduring, and limitless grace, mercy, and favor that I took command today (hell, that I even still have a career). It is also a testament to the love of all of my friends and family that kept me going while I struggled, fought, and trudged on to this point.

A couple weeks ago I wrote about how I was nervous about my transition since the guy I was taking over for didn't care for me too much. Well, guess what? I learned something. I learned a whole lot of something. I learned to never judge a man before you judge him for yourself. I learned that perception (and rumor and word of mouth and many, many other "ands") and reality can be very two different things. I learned what it meant to be a professional and put the mission and the men above your personal feelings. The outgoing guy said it best: "There is no room for personality conflicts between leaders." The transition was a dream. He taught me more than I ever hoped about leadership, command, management, our area of operations, and human dynamics. When the Squadron Commander told me today "Ok, it's all you now," the outgoing guy replied with "Sir, it's been all Terron for at least the last five days now. All we're doing is making it official." When he said that, I realized that, yes, in fact I had been running the show for nearly a week without realizing it based on the way he had handled the transition.

Fare thee well, brother, and good luck on your next assignment.

The last couple weeks have been an amazing experience that opened my eyes in countless ways. I had dinner with a Mujahedeen Commander who kept peacocks and ostriches as pets (and a monkey that fed him nuts), told me stories of him and his buddies fighting the Russians when I was still learning to crawl, and was basically Don Corleone in a man dress and turban. I met an ANCOP Colonel with the world's greatest mustache (seriously, think Burt Reynolds in the 70s) who engaged me in religious philosophy for two hours over dinner. There was the young sub-district manager (think city council member) who was full of fire and ideas and frustrated with red tape. There were the police commanders in our area, one who came up through the professional education system and the other the cousin of the Provincial Chief of Police. Both are as different as could be. The first wants nothing more than to be a good policeman. The second is little more than a thug with a badge, dreaming of the big score. I've got Lester Freeman from *The Wire* on one side and Vic Mackey from *The Shield* on the other. Most importantly, I rediscovered my passion and my love for my job. I feel like a Soldier again.

I'm sitting here at one end of this thing eyes wide open. I know this is just the beginning. I know the hard times are coming. I know that command will bring a mix of joy, pain, triumph, mistakes, laughter, and tears. I know this won't be easy. I know it's going to downright suck at times and all I'll want to do is throw in the towel. Today has been one of the greatest days in my career, but I know this is just the beginning. Tonight, I'll sit with my First Sergeant, smoke a cigar, and look to the future… because in the morning, the test truly begins.

P.S. Time till the first Soldier used the open door policy: 4 hours. Is this why they call command a "joyous burden"?

### Email: August 19, 2012

Days in Command: 17
IEDs found: 4
IEDs detonated: 2
Outposts closed: 1
Article 15's: 1 x company grade, 1 x field grade
Summary Court Martials: 1
Dinners with Afghans: 6? 7?
Green on Blue Attacks: 5 (or was it 8?)
Promotions: 1
Ass Chewings Given: 3
Ass Chewings Received: 1
New LTs received: 1
Red Cross Messages: 1
Emails received from the FRG: I stopped counting
Times I've wanted to choke a Soldier(s): 12
Times I've been incredibly proud of a Soldier(s): 6
Visits from the Brigade Commander: 1
Visits from my Squadron Commander: 4
Times I impressed the Brigade Commander: 1
Times I've impressed the Squadron Commander: I'll let you know when it happens
Times I've signed something: Please make it stop!
Meetings: I don't want to think about it.

    It's been a busy couple of weeks for me. It's been a slow couple of weeks for the Troop. It's weird how that works. Day to day has been a much slower pace than staff. I wake up when I want, go down when I want, work out when I want, break when I want. I'm the boss. At the same time, all those "wants" are put in check by the enemy, Squadron, Afghan partners asking me to dinner or calling to discuss "issues", my own Soldiers, paperwork, people needing my decision, and the list goes on. Command has been busy, tiring, frustrating, exhilarating, and depressing all at the same time.

I've had some amazing experiences in the last couple of weeks. I had dinner with a Mujahedeen Commander. Patrolled through the Afghan countryside which is surprisingly green and beautiful in places. Eating dinner with an Afghan Police Commander trying not to be obvious about counting hands and weapons or thinking about the fire team I have tucked 50 feet away ready to bust in if something happens. Watching the Afghan Police Commander wearing the same bored and tired look on his face as me while we sit in a joint meeting with our bosses. Laughing and joking with Afghan Police over how the military experience is pretty much the same regardless of the military you're in. Climbed to the top of a castle that once belonged to Alexander the Great so we could reenlist a Soldier. Inventorying one of my outposts and finding a room packed with explosives... including six old, decaying sticks of TNT.....

In the past couple of weeks I also turned 29 and enter the last year of my "youth." Pulling a muscle in my back yesterday doing squats gave me some time to think about the last 29 years. First off, I've concluded that my body is NOT 23 anymore, which means stretching before I exercise and no longer treating it like a rental. By 30 I will have graduated college, deployed three times, fought in and lead men in two separate theaters (OIF and OEF), and been in command of a unit. Oh, and I'll have gotten married. I've done and seen some amazing things in my life. I've met great people along the way. There's been hurt and there's been a lot of joys. All in all, not too shabby. I look around at my friends and it's weird to think that we're adults now (despite the best efforts to the contrary of some... like myself...). Strangely, I'm excited. They say life starts at 30, although I was always sure that was something people turning 30 said to comfort themselves. Either way, I'm stealing it. Seriously though, I feel like my life is truly taking off, and I can't wait to see what it holds.

I know this is a little rambling, but I hadn't written in a while and the combination of an all morning meeting, a massive "To Do" list, and the muscle relaxers for my back all left me a tad fried. Three and a half months down, five and a half to go.

## Email: September 27, 2012

Me: I'm worried about tracking them to the source.
LTC X: Yeah, well, I'm worried about them getting an IED in and it going off.
Me: I've got that covered. I wouldn't worry about it.

"Every day I put on my uniform and walk out that door there is a chance I won't come home"
–My Dad, a police officer of over 26 years.

Bahran is dead because of me.

Wait.

Stop.

Back up.

At the start of September western Kandahar City, the area I'm responsible for, decided this would be a good time to erupt. For about a week we had stuff blowing up every night. It wasn't us they were after. Attacks against

Coalition personnel in Kandahar City stay rather low. It does no good. The Taliban will not run us off. They aren't going to co-opt any of us. They won't get us to stop patrolling. Often we're too hard a target, even on our COPs. The juice isn't worth the squeeze. No, the target here is the Afghan Uniform Police (AUP), part of the Afghan National Security Forces (ANSF). Kill, intimidate, co-opt.

I never worked closely with Iraqi Police back in Baghdad. The majority of it was at our JSS where we kind of lived side by side and barely interacted. Here, we live, work, and patrol next to each other. You form relationships with them. They become people instead of "Afghans" or "AUP." Over at PSS 13 I worked with LT Mirwais, the Commander. Mirwais was an interesting guy. Half the time he pissed me off and half the time he made me laugh. I remember hanging out with him at PSS 13, eating lamb, smoking cigarettes, him trying to convince me to give him stuff (most notably an American pistol), and me trying to convince him I'd give him whatever he wanted for enough lamb. I remember standing next to him on Highway 1 the second night I took command as we watched his men clear a scene from a recent IED blast.

LT Bahran was Mirwais' Executive Officer. Bahran was a small, quiet guy. He had six kids. Not surprising for an Afghan, but surprising for, well, Bahran. Never expected so many kids from such a tiny dude. He was the brains behind PSS 13, the only one literate and possessed an easygoing, likable demeanor making him popular with both his fellow police and Coalition Forces. Bahran handled the logistics, the paperwork, and when Mirwais would lose his temper or throw a tantrum (which was about once a week), Bahran was the one you could count on to mediate. Both of them had worked hard to become police, going through all the formal training that the Afghan Police system offered. They had worked for their rank and hadn't "achieved" it through nepotism. Both loved being policemen, and both adamantly believed that Afghans would solve Afghan problems, not the Coalition.

And now Bahran is dead.

It all started a few days before when Mirwais got himself blown up. One night, my CP spotted three men working near a culvert late at night. I sent a patrol to the area, and they found evidence the men were prepping the site for an IED. Unfortunately, the patrol could not catch the insurgents before my UAS lost them. I set up 24 hour surveillance on the site over the next few days hoping the insurgents would return so we could kill them outright. My Squadron Commander wanted to set up an OP. I argued that an OP would scare the insurgents off and blow our chance to kill them. The Squadron Commander was concerned the insurgents would get the IED in place. Still, he let me make the call. All was going well until Mirwais got himself blown up two days later.

Mirwais had responded to an IED blast on HWY 1. Turns out, the first blast was bait. While Mirwais inspected the blast site another IED exploded, wounding him badly, though still alive. I had to pull my surveillance from the culvert to monitor the blast site and responding patrols. As we were finishing up with Mirwais being injured, I had to make a decision. Do I send a patrol back up to clear the culvert, or do I keep watch from afar? I looked at all the factors: the number of patrols, both ours and AUP that had been through that area, the surveillance plan, and the short length of the surveillance gap. I decided against physically clearing again and monitor from afar. Besides, we had seen nothing that gave me the inclination to clear it again. It was basically 50-50, and I'd already tapped the Troop bare dealing with Mirwais being wounded.

And now Bahran is dead.

The next morning Bahran went on patrol. Since his truck was in the shop, he took Mirwais', a truck easily identifiable by the spare tire on the back of the cab. As he drove over the culvert an IED went off. The blast flipped his truck like a toy and killing Bahran and four other AUP. It was in the exact same place we'd been observing. The exact same place we'd cleared just a day before. The exact same place that, just hours ago, I had decided not to clear again, instead opting to try reacquiring the IED emplacers and follow them home. I made my decision, and a man is dead because of it.

Would clearing the culvert have prevented Bahran's death? Maybe, maybe not. You never know. We don't know when it was inserted since all eyes were elsewhere. What shocked me the most about the incident were two things: The first is that as a commander it was my call. All it took was an order from me and the culvert would have been physically checked, but I opted for a different strategy. I took a calculated risk. The second was how much Bahran's death affected me. I was worried and nervous for Mirwais while he was in the hospital. I was sick to my stomach when Bahran died. In Iraq I couldn't have cared less about Iraqis, a product of the extreme situation and my own ignorance. When I got here, Afghans were Afghans. But something happens when you stop seeing people as labels, religions, or ideologies. You find out you have stuff in common. You find out you both joined an armed service for the same reason. You find out they love their wife like you love yours. You find out that their supply system only issues clothes in too small or too large just like your Army's does. You find out they're people, like you. It affects you… and it should.

Bahran gave his life fighting for a better Afghanistan. He was dedicated to his job and his country, and the Afghan Police have lost a true talent. Well done, brother. Be thou at peace.

Three months to go.

### **Email: October 1, 2012**

Total number of Field Grade (MAJ, LTC, COL) Officers I've worked closely with (including BN CDRs): 29
Number of field grades I would serve with again: 8
% of total: ~28%
Number of Battalion Commanders I've served under: 4
Number of Battalion Commanders I would serve with again: 1
% of Total: 25%
Number of field grades I consider mentors: 3
% of total (28): ~10%


LTC X: "Why don't you tell me, and be completely honest, what issue you have with me?"
Me: "My issue, sir, is that you treat me like a dog, you've done it for over a year, you do it publicly, and you do it on a personal level. That's my issue."

    Teacher

    Mentor

    Example

I don't know if I've ever sat through an Army leadership class or OPD session without hearing those terms thrown around.

I don't know how many times I've looked to my leadership expecting to see those things and been horribly disappointed or utterly disgusted at what I found instead.

One of the big buzzwords in the Army these days is "toxic leadership." A toxic leader is aloof, arrogant, selfish, doesn't listen, a bully, and someone who creates a horrible working environment to where the unit's performance and morale suffers. While the Army was quick to respond with "this will not be tolerated" and the "we're doing all we can to fix this" talking points, toxic leadership is, by far, still very much an issue.

Growing up as cadets and young lieutenants, we constantly heard from senior officers how important senior officer mentorship is in developing young officers. We heard that one of the most important things we could do was find a senior officer (in our case a MAJ or LTC) to mentor us through our time in the Army. However, I, like most young LTs, quickly got hit with a hard dose of reality: Those men and women are far and few between. Most senior officers I met were average. Not bad, not good, just average. Some I met were clueless, inept, or weak. Many I met were vain, arrogant, and egotistical. A handful was so virulent, despicable, and toxic they destroyed careers and whole units. A few were men I looked up too. There were three, for me, that I call mentors and still reach out to today when I have a problem I can't figure it out.

Why only three? The numbers above were a limited sample. I can't remember every field grade I've worked with over 8 years (trust me, there were a lot more). In truth, the percentage is even smaller. I consider myself blessed to have met three; two which I will most likely keep in touch with my entire career... and probably wrangle into one of those contractor held "special assistant" jobs when I'm a general. However, I talk to many of my classmates, other Captains, and a few field grades who all bemoan never having a mentor or are still looking. Their cases are common.

Why is it that we, as an Army, put so much emphasis on mentorship (it's even a criterion on our Officer Evaluation Forms), but only pay it lip service? I was told plenty of times as a LT to seek out a mentor, but never once have I been charged by a senior officer to make sure I mentor my LTs in turn. Correction, when one of them screws something up, I'm asked about my mentorship, but it usually takes the form of "fix this problem with them so they don't screw up again." It's never about taking a vested interest in their growth and development as leaders, officers, and, most importantly, as people.

One thing I swore I would do as a commander is to mentor younger Officers. I want to be a good mentor like the ones I was blessed with. Maybe one day down the road they'll be writing me from some hell hole across the globe as a young Company Commander asking for advice. Maybe I'll just be an influence for a little while. But either way, it's my duty to teach and mentor the next generation of officers as best as I can. In fact, the greatest mistake that my classmates, peers, and I can make is to complain about our lack of mentors, yet fail to turn around and pick up the next generation. We owe it to them, ourselves, and the Army.

In other news, the deployment rolls on. Work, sleep, fight with my boss, and say prayers of thanks this deployment has remained uneventful and boring. Well, we got to drop a couple of bombs on IED emplacers. We were watching the feed in our CP and broke out in cheers when we got them. As my XO said: "It was as if for one glorious moment, we were all fans of the same team, and that team just scored a game winning touchdown." One of my platoons (with a Platoon Leader so new that he still smells of mother's milk and baby powder) is out west doing an air assault mission with another battalion, so I've been sitting here like a worried parent with kids on their first trip away from home. Two and a half months left and then done. I can't wait. As my fiancée reminds me, apparently there's this wedding thing I signed up to do and have to get back for.

# Part IX:
# The Last Push

*Fucking Darvishan.*

*You always buy it on the last big mission.*

*We were starting to transition from operations to redeployment. Only a couple more weeks and we would start the downhill coast to packing up our equipment and getting on a plane.*

*And then, fucking Darvishan.*

*Word came down that another battalion in the Brigade needed help to clear a route and securing engineer assets. The engineers would build checkpoints to give the local AUP a more permanent presence. To make this happen I would lead a motley crew which included one of my recce platoons and my mortars, a recce platoon from my sister company, a National Guard engineer platoon, a route clearance package, and an SFAT team.*

*Fucking Darvishan.*

*The area of Darvishan we were moving through ran right into lower Baghak. Baghak was the site of our Squadron's large scale operation to confirm or deny suspected Taliban presence. Cav, we think there's enemy here. Go find them. That's what the Squadron did.... while we sat in Kandahar City minding the shop.*

*Now, my troop would get the chance for a big operation... right into Taliban country. One checkpoint we would put in was on a stretch of villages that had seen no permanent Coalition, Afghan Security Force, or Afghan government presence in nearly a year. The lone exception was our Squadron's foray into lower Baghak a month back. The Taliban ran the area lock, stock, and barrel. I was excited. I was nervous. If something bad went down this deployment, this is where it would happen.*

186

*Fucking Darvishan…*

## Email: November 10, 2012

We're entering the home stretch. This deployment was definitely not what I expected. Based on everything I'd heard about Kandahar City I expected a higher level of violence. Before I left I would tell people I was heading to Afghanistan, and they looked at me like I was just walking dead. I remember one girl who works at my Starbucks came from behind the counter, hugged me, and, with a rather heavy air of finality, said "Well, I will really miss seeing you." Hell, it was the same way at SRP on post. "Oh, you're going to Kandahar? Are you sure you don't need to update your will?" Seriously, that happened. So, although I haven't spent the deployment dodging bullets and have yet to fire my weapon in anger, this deployment has done wonders to give me a sense of fulfillment.

My first trip to Baghdad I was a little busy trying not to die, and things were rapidly spiraling downhill in Iraq at a breakneck rate. My second time in Iraq, I didn't have much of a front row view from Camp Liberty. This time, conversely, I can see the progress being made. We are winning, at least in our little corner of the war. I see the tangible results of our efforts. Afghan Police patrol on their own, take responsibility for security and (once we stopped giving them stuff) were quick to say they could do it without us. Most of the people I talk to have no love for the Taliban and don't want them back in power, and (once we stopped giving them stuff), turned to their government and the police for help. The government officials are finally gaining momentum down here, figuring out a working budget (once we stopped giving them stuff) and improving the area.

Recently, I was quoted out of context in two news articles. The part left out explained that even though tensions rise from time to time, we and the Afghans always work out problems TOGETHER. Since COL Farooq's been on leave I've been grateful for the quiet, but I kind of miss the cantankerous old bastard, especially his lamb. We get angry, we argue, but we always work it out over dinner, a cup of tea, and a laugh about how he keeps wishing me good fortune that Lauren bears me many, many man children.

Deep down, I think I always questioned the worth of these wars. I remember looking back to the friends, brothers, and classmates I've lost half way around the world and wondered if it mattered. I can now assuredly answer yes. I don't know what will happen in 10, 20, 30 years. This place could devolve into chaos again. I don't think it will EVER become the Jeffersonian Democracy we want, but that doesn't mean our efforts were wasted, that doesn't mean our lives were wasted, and that doesn't mean it was a hopeless endeavor. Whatever happens, I know one thing: for a time, we made things better, and for the guy climbing in the truck every day, or stepping off the bird on some mountaintop, or sitting down at yet another shura to drink even more chai, knowing you made it better, even if only for a little while, is all that matters.

### Email: November 24, 2012

"Camacho was taken off life support today, been in the news for at least 3 days. Do you know how many Soldiers were killed this week....of course not, they forgot to mention that in your local news." –A friend's Facebook status

"The death of one man is a tragedy, the death of millions is a statistic" –Commonly Attributed to Joseph Stalin

Total Service Members killed in Iraq and Afghanistan: 6,518

Total Service Members wounded in Iraq and Afghanistan: 41,936

When I was a Company Executive Officer in Iraq back in 2007, I remember seeing an article on CNN that made my blood boil. The article was about State Department personnel, particularly Foreign Service Officers (FSOs), who were being "involuntarily sent" to Iraq (translation: deployed) due to a critical shortage. FSOs responded with outrage. The quotes from the FSOs equated this to a "death sentence" (remember, Iraq was threatening to rip apart at the seams back then). The quote I will never forget was "This is cruel and unfair. Who will take care of my family if I'm killed or severely wounded?" What made my blood boil even more was how it was a common opinion (particularly amongst the State Department) that the U.S. military was nothing more than a 1000 pound gorilla trampling all over Iraq without the education, people, or skills to build a government (no shit) and that the war would better be served by the State Department running things with the military only on hand IF (ha ha ha) things were to start blowing up. Well, the State Department got their wish: full court press, everybody to Iraq... and they kicked, screamed, howled, and yelled how unfair it was to be put in harm's way. They weren't supposed to be in danger. They're diplomats, not SOLDIERS!

That was the rub. That's what pissed me off so much. Despite crying how much the military was screwing it up and how they needed to run things, they didn't want to be in harm's way, because they weren't Soldiers. We're not supposed to get hurt and killed, SOLDIERS are! It hit me like a ton of bricks. I wasn't exactly expendable, but I was pretty damn close. If I got killed or wounded society wouldn't react in horror, they'd shrug, say "what a shame" and turn on Jersey Shore. In Iraq, six men in my Battalion were killed in the same attack (four during and two died of wounds), their deaths reduced to a footnote on the CNN news ticker. When the Iraq War officially ended I didn't even see it on the front page of any major newspaper. I saw it in five minute flashes (if best) on local and cable news. The U.S. ending an eight year war wasn't even a major story. The local news in Olympia had it sandwiched between the traffic report and fucking gardening tips.

Our country will stop in its tracks for the next celebrity scandal, a new reality TV show, and a sporting event, but most people have no comprehension we have been at war for 11 years, and fighting in two theaters for eight of those. By the time it's all said and done (if you go with the 2014 exit as the "end") the war will have lasted 13 years. Major combat operations in Vietnam lasted 10. Most Americans can't even find Afghanistan or Iraq on a map. I've buried friends while the rest of the country turned the channel. Hey, *Dancing With the Stars* was on that night. I get it.

Before I left for this deployment, I was in downtown Olympia (one of the most hippie places in the country) at one of my favorite spots. I got my beer and just happened to sit next to two self-proclaimed intellectuals "discussing" America's "immoral wars." At one point, I turned and corrected some of their facts and then mentioned I had been to Iraq twice and was heading to Afghanistan, to which one replied "Now I know you're lying, because we're leaving Afghanistan, so why would you be going over there?" At that point I choose to return to my beer and my book, leaving her in her smug satisfaction of having "put me in my place." Shocking? Shouldn't be. The end of the Iraq War didn't even register for most people. Ask the average American what they remember about the War on Terror and they'll probably mention four events: 9/11, the invasions of Iraq and Afghanistan, and the death of Osama Bin Laden. What do I remember? I remember all those, I remembering reading about the Battles of Fallujah, dissecting the Thunder Run, following Operation Anaconda, the birth of COIN, the first body I pulled out of a street, stealing a kiss under a Baghdad moon, the first time I thought I would die, the first time I buried a brother, watching my life fall apart, watching our strategy actually WORK in Afghanistan, waiting EVERY DAY to hold my fiancée again.....

Every bullet fired in anger, every moment of terror, every drop of blood, and every tear of the past six years and three deployments etched itself into my heart and burned itself into my soul. But, for most, that translates to a blip (if any) in the news cycle and a passing recollection that a war goes on somewhere between *Jersey Shore* and the newest report on Lady Gaga's weight gain. It's cool though. They bought a yellow ribbon and support the Troops! ...wherever those Troops are going and whatever they may be doing.

## Email: December 24, 2012

Merry Christmas! Today marks my 4$^{th}$ Christmas deployed. Last night, I was checking on the guards and a young kid on his first deployed Christmas asked me about my first Christmas deployed. My first deployment, I had the "honor" of missing 2 Christmases. I remember "lighting" a cigarette off of a broken bulb on our Charlie Brown Christmas tree. I remember the giant inflatable Santa in front of our chow hall getting blown up by a mortar (or was that the second Christmas?). I remember the only thing I wanted for Christmas was to come back with all my fingers and toes.

This Christmas is a little different. I've been meaning to write for the last 2 weeks since I got back from running the IED gauntlet in Darvishan (a lot of stuff blew up over the course of those three days), but I kept getting overcome by events. Some highlights:

-Takes the Troop to Darvishan to build Afghan police a checkpoint. Nine IEDs over five kilometers. Afghan Police inform us it's too dangerous to stay at checkpoint and will follow us back. Stuff blows up, vehicles roll over, and a dog follows the Troop for three days becoming the mission's unofficial mascot.

- ANCOP Soldier threatens to kill U.S. soldiers. End up having sit down with ANCOP Brigadier General. Play politics for two days, drink tons of chai, admire ANCOP General's epic mustache, and finally manage to get the Afghan Soldier arrested.

-Get told ANCOP stole two pairs of NVGs during a layout and ANCOP rile against "false accusations". Eventually recover said NVGs two days later after showing ANCOP Commander video evidence. ANCOP Commander has thief publicly beaten before being hauled off for arrest. ANCOP Commander throws big apology dinner for my officers and myself. Somehow, I get talked into giving ANCOP Commander an elliptical machine as a thank you present.

-3$^{rd}$ Platoon runs over Afghan motorist who speeds out in front of a 55,000 lb. Stryker and then hit his brakes. Receive personal call from Brigade Commander. Division eventually determines accident was Afghan's fault.

Brigade Commander no longer demands I commit seppuku to atone for my myriad of failures.

-Attend memorial service for an advisor killed by a car bomb.

So yeah, I've been busy. Real busy. Command has to be the best and single MOST frustrating job I've ever had. I guess it's sort of like being a parent. You can talk to your guys until you're blue in the face, put control measures in place, and give orders out the ass, but you can't control all their actions. They'll still do stupid stuff (like run over a sensitive item... but I digress), and then you have to clean it up. It's also frustrating because of the war's politics.

At this point in the war it's all about preserving the relationship with the Afghans. As a result, when anything happens one of the first concerns is how/whether an event will damage that relationship... even if the circumstances were the Afghan's fault. The death threat and the theft lead Brigade to accuse me of "damaging" my relationship with the ANCOP. If you ask the ANCOP Commander he will tell you our relationship ended up stronger because of how we handed it. Same with the traffic accident. Even though the driver pulled out at the last minute in front of a vehicle with no hope of stopping, it was our fault. I can give you a thousand more stories where our Afghans partners lied to us, stolen from us, instigated fights, and MURDERED U.S. soldiers, and the first question is what we did to cause it.

There is an automatic presumption of guilt. Before the facts of the traffic accident came out I was told by a senior Officer that the Platoon's story was bullshit. He "knew" they were being reckless, they were driving too aggressively, were "lying" about their speed, and had "plenty of time and space" to stop a 55,000 pound vehicle... and he told me this off of the initial report, with no facts, no pictures, and no evidence. I was also instructed to "handle my shit" before he handled it for me. It took my XO laying out the math and measurements, along with pictures to prove that we weren't at fault. We were guilty until we proved our innocence. Even then, it was only grudgingly accepted after my XO worked out and diagrammed a physics problem.

When the Afghan threatened to kill us I went through a grueling period of having to explain that my Soldiers had reacted the way they'd been trained, the last time they were trained, and how the way I responded to the threat was in line with every tactical directive from Corp down... because an ANCOP Soldier (a known hash and opium junky who we'd had issues with numerous times before), popped off at the mouth. However, we were the ones who went through the inquisition and then accused of "damaging the relationship", the same relationship they've used to extort money from us, murder our Soldiers, blame us for their corruption, and then claim it's because we disrespect their culture, justifying their actions.

We have not been perfect in this war. Nowhere close. There are multiple examples of us trampling over Afghans because of a sense of "American Superiority", and neither is every Afghan corrupt. The new ANCOP Commander here is a great man, and I enjoy spending time with him, unlike the guy he replaced. The other night he took me to school in chess, and graciously allowed me to move my pieces back out of obviously bad moves, even as he toyed with me, chased me around the board, and whittled me down to nothing. Side note: chess is huge here. Never knew that. So what is the point? The point is that we are at "that juncture" in the war. Everything has strategic impact, and tactical and operational losses have to be accepted if they preserve the strategic end state. It's ugly, it's distasteful, and it's hell for the people at the pointy end of the stick, but here's a secret. The war isn't about us.

War is political will implemented through force. We all love war stories, we all love to cheer for the little guy, the private in the trenches, the Sergeant kicking in a door, and the Officer leading the charge over the hill. Guess what? Here's a hard truth that no one wants to say: None of that means shit if the strategic end state is not accomplished. Is it right? No. Is it fair? Not by a long shot. You want to talk about fair? We all say that life isn't fair. War, by comparison, makes life look perfectly fucking balanced.

So here I am, juggling flaming glass balls and new born babies while walking a tightrope over a shark tank, where one wrong move results in my death or injury, the death or injury of one of my soldiers, or even put the entire U.S. effort in Afghanistan at risk. While you're doing this colonels and generals on the other side of the battlefield drill down on you when something goes wrong, sharp shoot your actions, ask why you weren't in compliance with section 15, paragraph 5f, revision 4.7 of the latest policy memo or tactical directive. These are the rules now, and you deal with them or you fail in one way or another.

This isn't a gripe. This isn't a pity party. This isn't "feel sorry for me" or a plea for sympathy. This is just the stark reality of where we are in the war. How do we deal with it? We don't think about it. Politics will play out how they will. Some days you're the hero, some days you get served up. You have no control over it. What you have control over is your attitude and what you do every day. That's what we focus on. We take care of each other. We wake up, put our kit on, and get to business. We keep going. Despite all the doom and gloom that surrounds this war, we've made a difference. I see it every day. We have no time for politics. We have a war to win.

# Part X:
# Whole Again

*We established two Afghan Police checkpoints in Darvahsan and Lower Baghak.*

*We cleared nine IEDs in a five kilometer stretch. Four vehicles hit IEDs, multiple vehicles roll overs, and six Soldiers evacuated between the engineers and the route clearance guys. We caught three AUP conducting site prep for an IED and intercepted traffic of a failed IED ambush near the riverbed... and by intercepted traffic I mean I listened to them talk about me standing and talking to one of my Platoon Leaders.*

*It was a chaotic mess.*

*It was also a complete success.*

*We breached an enemy IED belt, put the Afghan Police checkpoints in, established a government presence, showed the Taliban they can't keep us out, and we brought everyone back with all their fingers and toes. All injuries were minor and all the injured soldiers finished the mission.*

*I could do it. I could lead men in combat again, have everything go to shit around me, and not fall apart. I could do it.*

*I could do it.*

## Email: January 30, 2013

"War...War never changes" –The *Fallout* Series

"Only the dead have seen the end of war." - George Santayana

Dad: "There's a whole group of Soldiers now that this (war) is all they've done their whole time in, the only thing they've known as adults"
Me: "Yeah, I know. I'm one of them."

    I'm sitting here in my apartment, two weeks after I got home, and writing what will be the final entry of my deployment story. It's a misconception that deployments end when you step on the plane to leave the war zone. Bullshit. Deployments end once you get back to normal. For some, the deployment never ends.

    The first time I came home was an utter disaster. Honestly, looking back I'm amazed it took nine months to self-destruct and didn't happen sooner. I won't go into too much detail, but in nine months I saw my entire life crumble before my eyes and had to start over. I didn't understand how to deal with it outside of drinking too much, running wild, and finding creative mixtures with the wide variety of pharmaceuticals the Army kept shoving at me in hopes I would just go away and stop asking for help.

    The second time I came home wasn't really much better. I was still a mess from my first deployment. I was waiting for a girl who never showed and decided to see just how fast and loose I could live. Looking back to those days it's amazing I came out with a functioning liver and didn't come out with random children... and that stage lasted until about April of 2012.....

This time it's different. It doesn't feel like I ever left. Seeing Lauren again was just like coming home after a long field problem. Going to the places I used to, slipping back into my old life, it's all been relatively easy. I haven't gotten blind drunk, I haven't made bad choices, and I could even do my grocery shopping without a mental breakdown or verbal outburst. You may laugh, but those who've deployed before know what that one's like. Something changed. I was more experienced. I grew up. I'm a commander and people depend on me to keep it together... but there was more to it than that.

Before I left, I was scared out of my mind. I'm not joking. I'm not talking a little nervousness. I was convinced I would die horribly, and violently. You have to understand, before I left word was that Kandahar City was on the tipping point and we could face potential huge levels of violence, violence akin to my first deployment. I don't know how I got on that plane. It was probably years of obedience drilled into me and the fact that once my feet moved I didn't stop and think about it until I was on a C-5 headed to Kandahar Air Field. Deep down I was NOT ready to go back to combat. Like my dad told me, the first time I didn't know any better and now I do. I knew what combat was like and the huge physical, mental, and emotional cost it could take from you. I was terrified of dying, but more than that I was terrified of coming back broken, physically or mentally, and putting Lauren through that... or if she'd even be there at all. Every nightmare scenario went through my head before I got on that plane. I cried myself to sleep with worry and, a couple times, got stupidly drunk. My life was coming together and I didn't want to die.

But something happened downrange. I didn't just finish this deployment, I finished three. This deployment was like therapy. We had a combat mission. I conducted patrols. I led a large out of sector mission where we took contact... but nothing horrible happened. I was pretty convinced I would bite it in Darvishan (nothing like nine IEDs in four or five kilometers), but the IED strikes we had resulted in nothing more than minor injuries. It was like therapy. I can deploy, I can fight, and I can get through it without coming apart. I'm strong enough to do this. With that realization, I laid down my ghosts. I finally, FINALLY put East Baghdad to bed and coming home to Lauren put down the loneliness of my second departure and homecoming. It was finally over. In nine months, I got myself back. It was over. I reached the end. I'm at the end of my war.

This war, for better AND worse, has defined me as an adult, a soldier, and a man. I joined the Army on July 2, 2001, when the West Point Class of 2005 took our oath on R-Day. Two months later, my world changed forever on September 11, 2001. It wasn't a question of IF I'd ever see combat, but WHEN. Everything at West Point was preparing for war. Everything as a lieutenant was training for war. Deploy, train, deploy, train, and deploy again. I will turn 30 this summer and all I have known my entire adult life is war. You know what scares me more than war? Peace. I don't know what a peace time Army looks like. I don't know what they mean by limited budgets or not being able to train how I want or need to because we "don't have the money." I don't know what I'll do or how I'll feel when, in eight months, there are no deployment orders or a slot for my unit on the patch chart. I know THAT. I know year on, year off. I know how to communicate how important training is because this shit goes live in a few months. I don't know peace. I don't know garrison. Among our profession there has been a lot of talk about defining our new role, of restoring institutional competency, and getting "back to basics."

Translation: we, as an Army (and to a broader extent the military in general), have forgotten everything about being a garrison time force. All we know is counterinsurgency and deployments.

All I know is counterinsurgency and deployments. I turn 30 in August and have been in the operational Army since Jan 2006. Since then, I have deployed to Baghdad twice and Afghanistan once. I've led men as a Platoon Leader and Company Executive Officer in Baghdad and as a Troop Commander in Afghanistan. They gave me medals in exchange for bits of my sanity and soul. I've fought in two separate theaters (or two separate wars depending on how you define it). It is HIGHLY unlikely I will be back over in either country in the foreseeable future. The war is over for me. My overriding emotion is relief. No more getting shot at, blown up, sleeping upright in vehicles, living out on COPs, no more being away from indoor plumbing... Still, part of me will miss it. Just you and the boys out in bandit country doing the Lord's work, swapping stories, smoking cigarettes, and watching illum rounds from the howitzers light up the night. There's something beautiful about it that's hard to express.

When I was a young lieutenant, all I wanted was to be a badass. I wanted to get in gun fights, hop fences, and kick in doors. I look back at my younger self with nothing but an overwhelming desire to slap the shit out of him. I'm looking forward to what is really important. In May, I get the privilege of marrying the love of my life and starting a family together. While I will miss my war, I look forward to a new chapter, a better chapter, one I wasn't always sure I'd reach and one I'll cherish every day. I still have 20 or more years or so to go in this uniform. I'll likely go to war again one day, but it will never be MY war like this one was.

Not even close.

*Halfway down the road to Hell,*
*Betwixt the sand and fire,*
*I found a place of blood and tears,*
*And we called it Rustamiyah.*

*A little further down the trail,*
*Across the mountains far,*
*I laid my pain and ghosts to rest,*
*In a place called Kandahar.*

Honor and Courage…

Courageous and Faithful…

Blood over Surrender…

# **Epilogue**

I was a High Risk Soldier.

Let me say that again.

I WAS a High Risk Soldier.

Despite what it may feel like or appear, PTSD does NOT have to be permanent. Neither is it something to be ashamed about. We don't shame people with the flu, a broken limb, or cancer. PTSD is just as real as those, and just like those other illnesses it can be treated and beaten.

You can beat PTSD.

This book isn't here to highlight what I did during deployment. It doesn't exist to talk about my career. It doesn't exist to get me a pat on the back or a beer bought at the bar. People may get the impression that I blamed the Army for what I went through. I don't. The Army isn't perfect. It has its share of problems, some of them serious, but I love the Army. All I ever wanted to be, and still want to be, is a Soldier. While the Army and Army leaders failed me at times, both the Army and Army leaders helped me overcome my problems.

I also don't blame Sara. Don't get me wrong, I was angry at her for years, but I then I recognized a hard truth. Yes, what I went through was tough, but how difficult do you think it was for her? It's heartbreaking to watch someone you love go through what happened to me yet be unable to do anything to help. She had to watch, day by day, as I went from the man she fell in love with to someone she no longer recognized. What would you have done? I would have left me too. Our relationship wasn't healthy for either of us. That was the hard truth: I made the choice to attempt suicide. No one forced me. I decided. I had to take personal responsibility. It wasn't until I stood up and said "I don't want to be like this anymore and I will change" that true progress began.

It doesn't matter what other people do or fail to do, how many doctors you see or therapists you talk to, or how many pills you pop. No one gets better until they choose to get better. All of those things have their place in helping you overcome your pain, but that's all they are: tools. The solution is a conscious decision and commitment to change and get better. Once that decision is made, find the tools that work for you, whether that's counseling, medication, charity work, talking to a chaplain, or some creative outlet.

I did not beat my PTSD on my own. I had bosses and Army leaders encourage me, invest in my potential, and made sure I was placed in the jobs I needed to continue advancement. They saved my career. I had friends who helped put me back together by listening without judgment, using tough love to call me out on my self-destructive behavior, and providing constant encouragement. I thought I was on my own and no one cared, but I had an incredible support network right in front of me once I opened my eyes. You may feel alone, but there is always someone ready to help once you ask.

The process isn't quick. It took five years after the end of my first deployment to feel like I had truly beaten my PTSD. There were so many times I wanted to quit, give up, and die. Also, this fight isn't a one-time thing. There are days I still get down, still struggle with depression. Now and then I'll still get a flashback or a nightmare… but there's a difference now. I know what these things are. I've developed healthy coping mechanisms: writing, visualization, exercise, or talking to someone if need be. I don't run from it or distract myself, but I confront it head on, immediately, not giving it a chance to take root again. I still carry all those horrible moments I experienced and I always will. The key is those moments went from something traumatic, to a bad memory, to just a memory.

Instead of letting this experience dominate me, I've used it to strengthen myself and influence my outlook for the better. This experience gave me the ability to empathize with others struggling with depression and suicide. It's led me to advocate for soldiers seeking treatment and ensure their privacy is protected. It's given me a passion to share my story, whether one on one, in a group, or, well, in a book. Most of all, my struggle has imparted a single, critical message.

You can beat PTSD.

Life will get better if you keep going.

This book is about telling the story of what doesn't get talked about.

This book is to give encouragement to anyone else going through the same thing in silence.

This book exists to give hope.

If I can make it, then you can make it too.

Don't give up.

Keep fighting.

It WILL get better.

You can make it.

You WILL make it.

I was a High Risk Soldier… and I am still standing.

# Acknowledgements

First and foremost, I thank God for protecting me in Iraq and Afghanistan and protecting me from myself back home. Even in my darkest moments, God placed people around me to pick me up, pull me along, and help put me back together.

I have to thank my wife second because if I don't I'll find myself sleeping on the couch. Writing a book is difficult. Writing a book about the worst period of your life is harder. Writing and publishing a book that lays your darkest secrets naked before the world is damn near impossible. Thank you, baby, for the encouragement, reassurance, and support.

A big thank you to Anna Friederich-Maggard and Donald Wright at The Army Press. They were invaluable in this process, connecting me with the right people, resources, and mentorship to make this book a reality.

To Dan and Christy Keating, thank you for always being there. Thank you for always encouraging, never judging, and for your steadfast and unconditional love and support.

Thank you to everyone who read and gave me feedback, especially MaryAnne Sommer. Also, thanks to Lisa Lykins, Greg and Liv Isham, Brian Walker, and Adam and Jordan Miller for providing early feedback.

A special thanks to Matt Runyan for reading everything I've ever written. Everything. I started working on this way back in 2008 when it was called "A Requiem for Innocence." I got serious about it in 2013 and called it the "The War Diaries." A couple years later it was "My

War." Whether it was a letter, a new piece, or minor edits spread across a hundred pages, Matt has always made time to read my work and give feedback. He has helped me rework countless (and I mean countless) drafts and rewrites. This book would not exist without you, your efforts, and your input. No, really, I'm too poor to afford a professional editor.

To Dr. Oscar Underwood, thank you for your encouragement and helping me find the courage to publish.

To my parents, Richard and Sandra Wharton, thank you for all the sacrifices you made raising and nurturing me. Most important of all, thank you for always making sure I knew I could always come home again. I know I'm horrible at calling and I only visit once a year, but you've always made it clear that I can always come home if I need it.

# **Glossary**

**1SG:** First Sergeant

**AAFES:** Army and Air Force Exchange Service

**AFB:** Air Force Base

**AUP**: Afghan Uniform Police

**BIAP:** Baghdad International Airport

**BN:** Battalion

**BDE:** Brigade

**CDR:** Commander

**CITV:** Commander's Independent Thermal Viewer

**CO:** Company

**COL:** Colonel

**CONOP:** Concept of Operation

**COP:** Combat Outpost

**CP:** Command Post

**EFP:** Explosively Formed Penetrator

**FOB:** Forward Operating Base

**FRAGO:** Fragmentary Order

**FSO:** Foreign Service Officer

**HE:** High Explosive

**HQ:** Headquarters

**IED:** Improvised Explosive Device

**JAM:** Jaysh al-Mahdi

**JSS:** Joint Security Station

**KAF:** Kandahar Airfield

**KIA:** Killed In Action

**LOGPAC**: Logistics package. Commonly known as resupply

**LPD:** Leader Professional Development

**LT:** Lieutenant

**LTC:** Lieutenant Colonel

**MAJ:** Major

**MRE:** Meal Ready to Eat

**MP:** Military Police

**NBC:** Nuclear Biological Chemical

**NCO:** Noncommissioned Officer

**NTC:** National Training Center

**OBC:** Officer Basic Course

**OER:** Officer Evaluation Report

**OP:** Observation Post

**OPD:** Officer Professional Development

**PL:** Platoon Leader

**PSG:** Platoon Sergeant

**PSS:** Partnered Security Station

**PT:** Physical Training

**PX:** Post Exchange

**R-Day:** Reception Day

**RIP:** Relief in Place

**RPG:** Rocket Propelled Grenade

**RTE:** Route

**S3:** Operations Officer

**SFAT:** Security Force Assistance Team

**SFC:** Sergeant First Class

**SIGACT:** Significant Activity

**SITREP:** Situation Report

**SQDN:** Squadron

**SRP:** Soldier Readiness Processing

**SSG:** Staff Sergeant

**TOA:** Transfer of Authority

**TOC:** Tactical Operations Center

**UAS:** Unmanned Aerial Surveillance

**VBC:** Victory Base Complex

**XO:** Executive Officer

# About the Author

Terron Wharton was born and raised in Fort Wayne, Indiana. His chosen military path began with joining his high school's JROTC program. His mother was not thrilled, but agreed as long as Terron kept his GPA above a 3.0. He first learned about West Point while in JROTC and became the first in his family to attend a service academy. He graduated in 2005 with a degree in International Relations and was assigned to Armor Branch, his first choice. In October 2006 Terron deployed to FOB Rustamiyah in Baghdad, Iraq as a Tank Platoon Leader, leading 16 men and four tanks in combat. This 15 month deployment occurred during "The Surge", a period marked by high levels of violence and viewed as a turning point in the Iraq War. Terron deployed two other times as part of the Global War on Terror. The second was to Baghdad again, this time as a staff officer to one of the largest Coalition bases in Iraq, Victory Base Complex. The third deployment was to Kandahar City, Afghanistan, during which he led over 100 Soldiers as a Troop Commander and lived with over 400 Afghan Police. Terron's time in Afghanistan changed his views on war as much as his first deployment formed them, becoming the driving catalyst behind this book. He presently resides in Leavenworth, KS with his family preparing for his next Army journey. *High Risk Soldier: Trauma and Triumph in the Global War on Terror* is his first book.

Made in the USA
Middletown, DE
12 August 2020